MiND JOGGER

A PROBLEM SOLVING COMPANION

miND JOGGER ®

HAL ZINA BENNETT

CELESTIAL ARTS
BERKELEY, CALIFORNIA

Registration in U.S. Patent and Trademark Office pending.
MIND JOGGER is a 🖐 PATH: Inner Resources book,
a series of tools for tapping the wealth of our inner worlds.

Cover Photography:
Prismatic Dispersions by Barbara Dorsey
Cover and Interior Design by Ken Scott
Typography by Ann Flanagan Typography

Made in the United States of America

First Printing, 1986

Library of Congress Cataloging-in-Publication Data

Bennett, Hal Zina, 1936–
   Mind jogger.

   1. Problem solving—Problems, exercises, etc.
2. Intuition (Psychology)—Problems, exercises, etc.
3. Mind Jogger (Game) I.Title.
BF441.B43   1986   153.4'3   85-28943
ISBN 0-89087-455-7

1   2   3   4   5   6   7   8   —   90   89   88   87   86

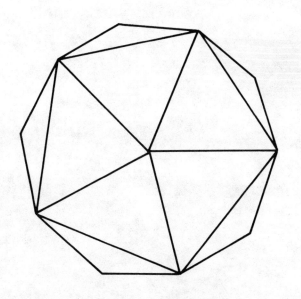

There is a time in every man's education when he arrives at the conviction that envy is ignorance; that imitation is suicide; that he must take himself for better, for worse, as his portion; that though the wide universe is full of good, no kernel of nourishing corn can come to him but through his toil bestowed on that plot of ground which is given him to till. The power which resides in him is new in nature, and none but he knows what that is which he can do, nor does he know until he has tried.

—Emerson

ACKNOWLEDGEMENTS

I want to thank the following people who helped in the birth of this book: David Hinds whose editorial expertise includes a rare talent for juggling intuition, vision, and logistics, while making it all look easy; Phil Wood who has translated his often challenged belief in the importance of the West Coast experience into a major publishing force; and George Young who far more than knowing the right answers, knows the right questions to ask. I also thank Paul Reed for editorial refinements that helped the book flow, Ken Scott for a stunning book design, and Ann Flanagan for her fine typography. Thanks to the unsung heros and heroines of Celestial Arts and Ten Speed Press whose attention to detail does not go unnoticed, though their names may never appear in the books they help make possible.

Last but not least, special appreciation to my son Nathan Bennett, the first to test Mind Jogger in its final form.

I dedicate this book
To Susan, my wife and soul mate:
Whose love and companionship on the
inner journey make the path glow;
And whose hand in mine
On the outer journey,
Brings a special comfort and joy
I have never before known.

▲

**TABLE
OF
CONTENTS**

M I N D J O G G E R

▲

BEFORE
YOU
BEGIN

Mind Jogger comes packaged with a 20-sided die with which
you will make selections from the readings contained on
pages 52–93. The die is an integral part of this system.

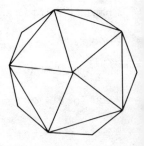

If you would prefer to make reading selections with cards, see instructions and charts for this method on page 156. Charts are provided for both ordinary playing cards and the Rider Waite Tarot deck.

The basic instructions for using Mind Jogger begin on page 24. You can start there, if you wish.

If you want to know more about the history, legends and theories behind Mind Jogger, start with the first chapter of the book, page 8.

Mind Jogger has numerous applications for both your private and professional life. In Chapter Three, page 38, I have described several applications that Mind Jogger users have suggested over the years. Turn to the Table of Contents for a comprehensive list of these applications.

The more you use Mind Jogger, and the more familiar you become with it, the more it will appear to **anticipate** your needs and provide you with highly relevant information. The readings the die **randomly** selects will seem too much on target to be merely coincidental. C.G. Jung referred to this phenomenon as **synchronicity,** which he defined as "an acausal connecting principle." When this occurs, as it inevitably does when people use Mind Jogger regularly, the work you do with this little book will become increasingly powerful and valuable in your life. Welcome this moment as a real turning-point, easing the burden of every important decision you may encounter.

The 20-sided die is an important part of Mind Jogger. If you want additional dice of this kind, they can be obtained from most game supply stores and stores that carry supplies for "Dungeons and Dragons" and other "role-playing games." Dice can also be obtained by contacting: **Koplow Games, 369 Congress St., Boston, MA 02210, (617) 482-4011.**

▲

THIS IS MORE THAN A BOOK,
IT'S A
BRAINSTORMING
COMPANION

Think about problems you have solved in the past and you will
　　　probably discover that as you approached the resolution
　　　there was a breakthrough moment, an exciting and fertile
　　　moment when the pressures of the problem suddenly
　　　gave way to a flood of promising new ideas. How well
　　　the term "brainstorming" fits such experiences! Anxieties
　　　you might have felt disappear at that moment, as you
　　　entertain fresh alternatives.

For most people, brainstorming of this kind is a complete mystery.
　　　It just happens—or so it appears. There seems to be nothing
　　　one can do to get it started at will. For all intents and pur-
　　　poses it is outside one's voluntary control. But that is no
　　　longer the case, thanks to the book you now hold in
　　　your hands.

With Mind Jogger you can trigger the breakthrough moment
　　　in virtually any kind of problem. Once the process becomes
　　　familiar to you, the book will become a very trustworthy
　　　brainstorming companion. You may turn to it for help in
　　　solving problems just as you might turn to the comfort of
　　　a friend whose support and problem-solving abilities you
　　　have grown to trust. Although Mind Jogger can't replace
　　　the need for friendship, it can play that special role our
　　　best confidants play in helping us gain access to our
　　　own inner resources.

One of the first persons to test Mind Jogger was a friend of
　　　mine who was in the middle of a major career change.
　　　Alex had been successful in business, and for the most
　　　part knew how to enjoy his success. But he was bored
　　　and felt trapped by the daily routine of managing his
　　　business. Like so many entrepreneurial types, his real
　　　interests lay in the startup phase of business, not in
　　　the day to day routine of keeping the business going.

▲

After listening to his complaints over dinner, I gave my friend a crude first model of Mind Jogger. The following day he telephoned me from his office. "I can't thank you enough," Alex said. "I don't know how or why it works, but in half an hour with Mind Jogger I solved a problem that has been on my mind for months."

Alex related his entire story to me about how Mind Jogger had helped him. The problem he had addressed to it revolved around a personal dream that he shared with his wife. They wanted to buy an historic building in the Sierra Foothills and convert it to a very exclusive country inn. But he had felt that his present business responsibilities left him no time to pursue that dream, and that it would be impossible to find a competent person to take over some of those responsibilities so that he could take time off.

With Mind Jogger's help he was able to get focused on the key issue—his own anxiety about trusting his business to another person. Working with the book, Alex was able to see that his own fears—not the availability or unavailability of competent administrators—was preventing him from hiring a person to assume some of his business duties. He finally found and hired such a person and gave himself the time to spend with his wife putting together their dream.

I am also reminded of a friend who was having trouble with her teenager. Barbara complained that her son swore at her any time she made demands on him to come home at a certain hour or to help out with chores around the house. She had tried everything, from taking away privileges to reasoning with him. "No matter what I do," she said, "It seems to be the wrong thing. He just gets more rebellious."

After working with Mind Jogger, Barbara decided to trust her intuitive sense, that even though the boy was rebellious, he still needed, and in fact was seeking, the limits she tried to impose on him. She decided that she would con-

tinue to tell him what she considered to be acceptable
and unacceptable behavior.

She told me that her work with Mind Jogger allowed her to see
that: "I can't force him to comply, but I do have a responsibility to myself, if no one else, to let him know what I
find unacceptable, and I intend to do that with no apologies
to anyone."

In neither of these stories did Mind Jogger **prescribe** the
answers. Rather, it provided two key elements for solving
problems: First, it provided a safe structure for working
through the problems systematically; and second, it provided verbal clues—the brainstorming prompts, if you will—
which brought up information, stored in memory, that
the person had forgotten or which s/he had never translated into a practical course of action.

There are certainly new concepts to be learned from Mind Jogger.
And you will discover ideas that will seem fresh and new
to you every time you consult it. But for the most part it is
in Mind Jogger's capacity for helping you gain access to
your own hidden reserves of knowledge that the true
power of this system lies.

The heart of Mind Jogger is a collection of Texts and Guides
that you will find in the last half of the book. Each of
these is a mental key that will help you unlock information hidden in the furthest recesses of your mind. You will
discover in using Mind Jogger that you actually know far
more than you think you do. Not only will you discover
that your knowledge is much broader and deeper than
you thought, you will learn to assemble that knowledge
in new ways, generating new ideas from ideas that are
already familiar to you.

The principles of Mind Jogger are thousands of years old. The
general techniques are drawn from ancient "oracle" systems, such as the I Ching, Tarot, or the Viking Runes.
Mind Jogger differs from these earlier systems in that the
readings selected in this book are contemporary in content

▲

and style. In addition, its unique structure for applying the insights you'll get from Mind Jogger are derived from modern education and business management techniques. That structure gives Mind Jogger a practical function that truly makes it an important tool for solving problems and boosting creativity in every area of life.

On page 94, you will find the beginning of the Mind Jogger Journal. This section is included so that you can create a permanent record of your work with this problem-solving system. It is particularly valuable for creating your own Personal Journal, as described in Chapter Three. Once you have filled in these pages they become a valuable reference, reminding you of themes, inner strengths, and recurring issues that are integral to your life—specific inner resources that you bring to every challenge you confront in your life. You will find more about the use of this journal on pages 38 to 51.

I hope you will enjoy owning and using Mind Jogger, and that it will help make whatever paths you take in your life a little easier and a little more pleasurable.

MIND JOGGER

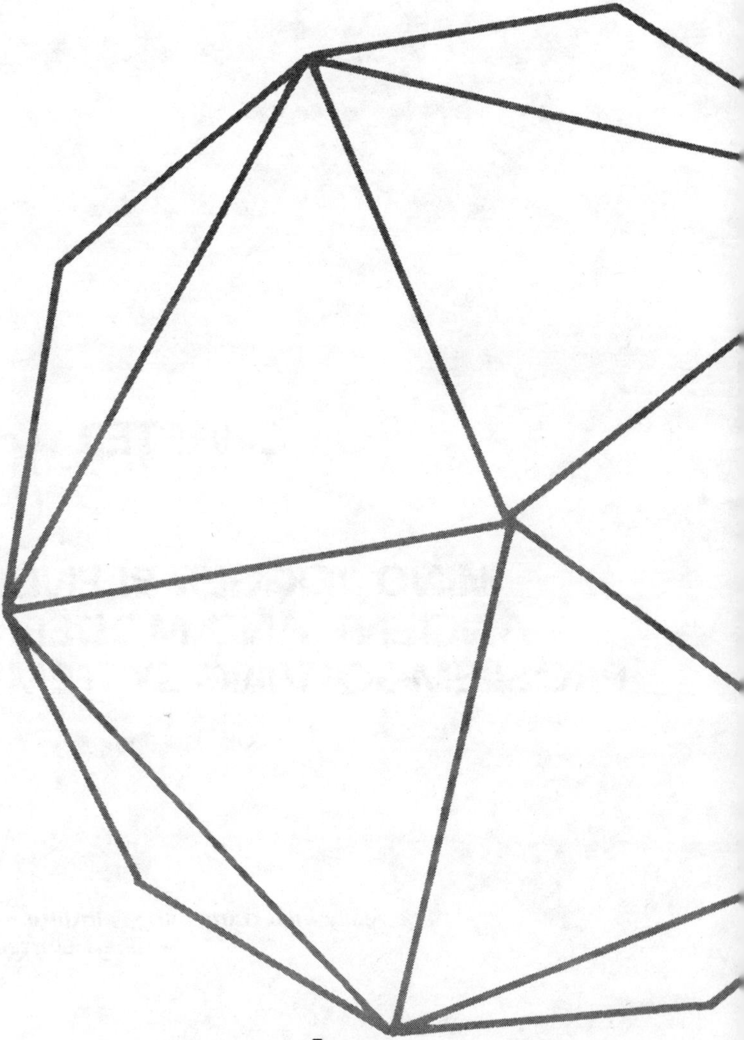

▲

CHAPTER 1

MIND JOGGER BLENDS ANCIENT AND MODERN PROBLEM-SOLVING SYSTEMS

"The really important thing is intuition."
—Albert Einstein

The idea for Mind Jogger came to me nearly fifteen years ago
at a time when I was looking for a problem solving
method that would expand alternatives and broaden possibilities rather than narrow or limit them. I wanted a system for dealing with everyday problems that would utilize
creative and intuitive processes, promising the excitement
of discovery at the same time that it provided a secure
guiding structure. I wanted to be able to link the familiarity of my own ideas with ideas that were fresh and new
to me, the way a conversation with a trustworthy friend
often does.

The fault I found with other problem-solving systems was
that they offered no element of discovery, no element of
the unexpected to "jog" my thoughts, to suggest a new
path that I might never find alone. Problem-solving systems such as outlining, prioritizing, and conflict resolution
helped me get my thoughts in order. They worked with
what could be clearly described—resolving, clarifying, putting issues into perspective. But in my own life, there
seemed to be only a few problems that yielded to that
kind of linear process. Most of the problems that cause
major concern require a much different method. My search
for that different method took me into some unexpected
areas of study.

A NEW LOOK AT AN ANCIENT TRADITION

When I was in my early twenties a friend who was studying
anthropology introduced me to the I Ching, the ancient
Chinese system of oracles. At the time we treated the I
Ching as a curiosity, a religious artifact from an ancient
culture, filled with mystery for both of us. Casting the
yarrow sticks or coins to randomly select the readings
contained in the Book of Changes often yielded thought-
provoking and even quite useful results.

I did not fully understand all the readings of the I Ching, and
more often than not, when I turned to it for help, I ended
up with a collection of contradictions and ambiguities that
left me as confused as when I started. Instead of helping
me to solve the problem I had on my mind, my readings
of the I Ching became diversions, not unlike reading inspi-
rational poetry in times of distress or doubt.

We knew only enough about Eastern philosophies—popular
books about Taoism were much in vogue with college
students at the time—to see that the I Ching could provide guidance through times of confusion or fear, when
one's first-hand knowledge and experience in life simply
weren't enough. But it also became obvious that unless I
was willing to devote hours to the study of the religious
tradition out of which the I Ching had evolved, this
ancient problem solving system would never be of
any use to me.

Even though it did not work for me as a problem-solving
system, the system of random selection which the I Ching
employed in the choice of readings continued to intrigue
me. At the time I didn't know exactly why I was intrigued. Years later when I began putting the Mind Jogger
together, I knew that random selection would somehow
have to be a part of it. My goal was to combine the
structuring methods of modern problem solving systems
with the thought-provoking methods of our ancient fore-
bearers. Many years later, while exploring different possibilities for Mind Jogger, I studied not only the I Ching but
also the Tarot, the Viking Runes, the Medicine Wheel of
the Plains Indians, and the Zuni fetishes, along with a
variety of goal-setting techniques associated with the psychology of behavior modification.

The most difficult part of the project, I quickly discovered, was
writing the Texts and Guides that would be the heart of
Mind Jogger. I thought it presumptuous, indeed, to under-
take such a venture, but I decided to give it a try in any

case. After all, I only wanted this system for my own use.
I could write whatever I pleased.

The first versions of Mind Jogger were crude. I typed the readings on 5 x 7 index cards which I shuffled and dealt out in a particular pattern, much as you'd do with Tarot cards. I gave sets of these cards to friends and business associates. In the process of using the cards people often thought of new ideas I might integrate into the program. Over the years I have added bits and pieces of friends' ideas or suggestions for changes into my collection of readings.

I have found ideas for the Mind Jogger readings in a variety of places—ranging from religious tracts to books on business management to my own creations. There were readings I tried that didn't work out, and these I quickly discarded. There were readings that turned out to be too specific or too prescriptive or too esoteric, which I also threw out. The readings as they now stand represent the best of the lot, winnowed out and refined over the years.

Because Mind Jogger combines the most modern research of the human consciousness with intuitive and creative techniques practiced by ancient cultures, people from all walks of life, and with widely varied interests, can find it helpful. To date Mind Jogger has been used by a wide range of professional people—from school teachers to nuclear physicists. And all have found it equally helpful in bringing the powers of the intuitive processes and their own creativity to the problems they face.

VISIONS OF SNAKES AND SWORDS
—PARADIGMS OF INTUITION AND CREATIVITY

In the study of the human mind, the story is often told of how Kekule, the 19th century chemist, discovered the structure of the carbon atom while researching the benzene molecule. Late one evening, after hours of frustrating work, he sat down to rest at his hearth. As he stared into the

glowing coals in his fireplace, he saw the image of a
snake with its tail in its mouth. He knew what he saw
was a hallucination, but as he studied this image, he
realized that it offered a solution to the problem that had
engaged him for months. The loop represented by the
snake suggested the structure of the carbon molecule.
The research that followed proved Kekule correct, and
this discovery resulted in a quantum leap forward for
the science of chemistry.

There is a similar story told about Elias Howe, the inventor
of the sewing machine, who received an unexpected
answer to a key mechanical problem when he dozed
off at his workbench and dreamed of a spear with an eye
in its tip. This image provided him with the idea for the
needle design that made the modern sewing machine
possible.

Many people have had similar experiences in their own lives,
getting answers to problems at unexpected moments. All
these experiences teach us that our most creative solutions
frequently come when we least expect them. Such experiences characterize what brain researchers commonly refer
to as intuitive and "non-linear" thought processes.

LIMITS AND STRENGTHS OF
LINEAR AND NON-LINEAR PROCESSES

There can be little doubt that non-linear processes have been
around far longer than the linear ones. Indeed, there are
those who argue that it has only been through a very
willful effort, and a powerful sense of inventiveness, that
the human race has come to the point of depending so
much on linear thought processes. Why then should we
need help with the non-linear? The answer to that is
found in our lifestyles.

Most urban dwellers now spend nearly 80 percent of their
waking hours communicating with other people, and this

communication demands the use of language and math, as well as complex, and usually unspoken, rules of behavior. In our daily lives we must deal with money, planning ahead, organizing the use of our time, understanding and conforming to rules governing the flow of traffic, to say nothing of organizing our minds in our professions. All these are predominantly linear activities. And in modern life we are so immersed in the linear that we have little time or energy to exercise our non-linear capabilities. It may well be that we now require a linear method to act as a bridge into the non-linear—which is where Mind Jogger comes in.

For most people, confusion is the most familiar part of any problem that doesn't yield to linear problem-solving techniques or to what is generally looked upon as "common sense." When problems are pressing, our minds seem suddenly to reel with an onslaught of disorganized material —numbers with no bottom lines, images of people and places, memories, feelings, fragments of advice from authorities and friends, vague or focused anxieties. All these swirl about in our minds, sometimes like gentle breezes, sometimes like storms, but nearly always in an unsettling way. Try as we might no single effort to make sense of these confusions seems to help.

RECLAIMING LOST POWERS OF THE MIND

In the past two decades there has been a push in human brain research to understand the non-linear workings of the mind. Even though the abstract understanding of these processes has been advanced, the practical skills for employing those findings have been slow in coming. We learn that the non-linear processes are apparently fragile and serendipitous, and there is a prevailing attitude that they are too delicate to control in any deliberate way.

13

▲

While the left brain has a preference for information that is closely related, or which can "fit neatly," one piece into another, the right brain has a preference for disparity and variety and is capable of juggling divergent and even conflicting bits of information. F. Scott Fitzgerald said that "The test of a first-rate intelligence is the ability to hold two opposed ideas in the mind at the same time and still retain the ability to function." This might well describe the special capacities of the right hemisphere of our brains.

Brain researchers agree that truly creative thought occurs when there is full co-operation between the two hemispheres, but with the right brain taking a dominant role. The co-operative effort includes the production of a "hologram," or three-dimensional image, within the brain. It is just such images that I spoke of earlier, in the cases of Kekule and Howe—that is, images that became integrating factors for divergent or seemingly conflicting pieces of information.

There is a strong link between the process described above and what we know of the intuitive and creative problem-solving processes. It has been speculated that creativity and intuition are strongest not when there is complete harmony between right and left brains but, on the contrary, when the two hemispheres are juggling conflicting or divergent materials. Bringing the hemispheres together, asking them to co-operate when they are seemingly in opposition, causes a sort of inner tension. This tension results in the creation or discovery of the hologram, which being of three dimensions, containing "depth" in addition to height and width, offers the opportunity for integrating a greater variety and number of thoughts and feelings than would otherwise be possible.

Working from the hologram, you are able to perceive new interrelationships between the various elements of information stored in the two hemispheres of your brain. And once an organizing image forms in this way, you can begin plotting a course of action that will bring together

14

all the elements with which, only moments before, you had struggled.

In the words of Albert Rothenberg, a researcher at Yale University School of Medicine:

> **The simultaneous presence of contradictory and conflictual elements…allows for new integrations and resolutions…**

To understand why the hologram increases the opportunities for processing information, compare the surface area contained in an artist's drawing of, say, a salad bowl, with the surface area of the real thing. Even if both are life-sized, the drawing still offers only a single flat surface, while the object itself contains inside and outside surfaces —depth in addition to height and width.

It is almost as though we can mentally wander around this hologram we create. It is not unlike what happens in a museum when you walk around a large piece of sculpture to view it. As you move around it you see many other surfaces besides those of the sculpture itself. Out of the corner of your eye, you may see a wall in the background, a stranger walking past, light and shadow cast along the floor. And seeing all these in relation to the curves of the sculpture, you see the common sights—the wall, the person walking past, light and shadows—all in new ways. It is as though the sculpture, for a moment, gives you new eyes to see. Shapes of the sculpture mingle with everything in your mind, reintegrating your perceptions so that you begin to expand your perceptions. The mental hologram works the same way—providing your "mind's eye" with a new way to see.

The hologram has one other important characteristic for mind researchers: In a hologram, a picture of the whole can be produced from any one of its parts. Thus, from any vantage point around the hologram, the mind "sees" not only that particular perspective but a picture of the whole as well. It is as if while standing at one corner of a building you could see not only that corner but the entire building, inside and out. The mental hologram, then, provides unlimited associations between whatever materials it calls forth in the mind.

Mind Jogger utilizes these brain processes by inputting new, often enigmatic information, ultimately triggering a co-operative effort between left and right hemispheres of the brain. The resulting tension, though usually subtle and gentle, forces us to leap out of the dominant left brain mode.

Information from the Mind Jogger can rarely be processed only through the efforts of the left brain, and so the right brain must rally to the cause. It is at this point, while both hemispheres struggle with this new input, that the hologram begins to take shape. And now we truly take that leap outside ourselves, finding solutions that can be astonishing both in their simplicity and in their effectiveness.

THE DILEMMA OF MENTAL DISCIPLINE

The human capacity for linear thinking has responded well to the steady reins of mathematics, physics, and the social sciences. But if the non-linear processes really are as precariously balanced as we think, wouldn't they be not simply tamed but dispirited by the harness of similar efforts to bring them under our control?

While linear processes respond well to a reining in, the non-linear processes respond best to a freeing up. In the words of poet Robert Browning, the latter process:

Rather consists in opening out a way
Whence the imprisoned splendor may escape...

Mind Jogger is a system for "opening out," for bringing the serendipitous powers of non-linear and intuitive thinking into focus. It is perhaps the first fully modernized solution to this ancient puzzle, here presented in a form that can be easily applied in every area of our lives.

THE ROOTS OF RANDOM SELECTION

The technique known as "random selection," that I've used in Mind Jogger—i.e. casting a twenty-sided die to select readings—dates back many thousands of years. The ancient Egyptians, Chinese, and the Vikings, and even the American Indians, have used systems employing random selection for finding solutions to a wide range of problems, from settling political disputes to mapping routes for open water navigation. And, of course, random selection occurs throughout nature. In genetics, for example, the random selection of genes makes it possible for new species to evolve and for there to be wide individualization of members within any species.

In the ancient Chinese traditions, random selection was not thought to be truly random or accidental. It was believed that everything in nature had a rhythm, a pattern. When the ancient Chinese tossed the yarrow sticks to make selections from the I Ching, it was believed that the sticks were responding not to chance but to a universal order. The readings that came up for each cast applied very specifically to the person who had cast the yarrow sticks at that moment in time and space.

In working with Mind Jogger over the years I have noticed, and others have reported, that on really important issues, especially with issues that keep coming up in a person's life, the selections do appear to come up the same more often than is mathematically probable. The explanations for this vary greatly. Some people theorize that we unconsciously control the die, causing it to come up with the same reading selections until we fully understand what we need to solve the problem. Others feel that the die is responding to a universal order, such as that believed

▲

to be so important with the I Ching. Whatever the explanation, it is a curious phenomenon, one that surprises me every time it occurs.

Systems that used random selection as a problem-solving technique often contained a collection of universal ideas and concepts, such as "harmony," "conflict," "action," and "patience." Usually, these were highly abstracted and philosophical. Because of their abstract qualities they could be applied to a wide variety of situations. Taken singularly, these ideas seldom had practical applications. But when joined together and applied to a specific problem they assisted the person who had selected them to re-think the problem. Then the person extrapolated information from what they had worked out, to formulate a practical application.

Like the Oracle at Delphi of ancient Greece, the readings supplied by these systems were not meant to foretell a person's future, as the popular press often describes; rather, they provided counsel. The counselee was expected to pay particular attention to the readings, but it was assumed that each person accepted the fact that he possessed a will of his/her own and that they had to take responsibility for their own destiny.

RANDOM SELECTION AND NATIVE AMERICAN CONCEPTS OF INTROSPECTION

According to Hyemeyohsts Storm, a Northern Cheyenne writing in **Seven Arrows,** the Plains People of the United States had a very sophisticated oracle system which they called the Medicine Wheel. The wheel was made up of rocks, each of which represented a creature or force in the physical and spiritual world. Everything in the wheel had a determined relationship with everything else in the wheel—except mankind. Humans, the Indians believed, had their own "determining spirits." That is, they were

18

free to explore and change and, to some degree, shape their own destinies. A person was considered to be trustworthy only when he had learned how to use responsibly his own determining spirit.

A person who lived in this culture—and believed in this system—acquired knowledge about himself through what the Plains People called a Vision Quest. To quote Hyemeyohsts Storm:

> We must all follow our Vision Quest to discover
> ourselves, to learn how we perceive of ourselves,
> and to find our relationship with the world around us.

Everything one thought and felt as he contemplated the Medicine Wheel was part of the Vision Quest and was seen as telling the person something about himself. Nancy Wood, who lived with the Taos Indians for most of her adult life, commented on this process in a poem, where she wrote:

> I take my eyes to some high place until I find
> A reflection of what lies deep within me.

If one goes deeply enough into the study of the various examples of random selection employed by ancient peoples, it becomes quite apparent that all of them began as carefully constructed mental disciplines aimed at making sense of the world in which they lived. Self-reflection was always a key element, and through such systems the individual could juggle "knowns" in the constantly shifting air of his own "determining spirit"—or as William James would have called it, "free will."

INTERPLAYS OF KNOWNS AND UNKNOWNS

Random selection makes the duplication of any one of the Texts or Guides of Mind Jogger all but impossible. Each time selections are made, information is assembled in a new and, usually, unexpected way. And yet, because one

▲

knows the general content of the readings (or certainly
will get to know them in time), one doesn't feel aban-
doned on wholly unfamiliar ground.

It is this combination of familiarity and unexpectedness that
makes the Mind Jogger system so valuable. Grappling
with universal mystery alongside the known, intuitive
processes are set in motion. One is encouraged to venture into the unknown, secure that there will always
be a mental "hand hold" within easy reach.

IS RANDOM SELECTION AN OCCULT SYSTEM?

Throughout the ages, there have been people who felt that
there was magic involved in random selection. Indeed,
some people claimed the power to forecast the future,
cure disease, and even cast spells on one's enemies. There
can be little argument that in many shamanistic societies
there are strong links between systems of random selection and psychic or mystical abilities. But there are schol-
ars, the great psychologist C.G. Jung among them, who
believe that systems of random selection were primarily
intended for "applying elite or esoteric knowledge in the
practical world."

In most cases the systems became associated with mysticism
only because they evolved in pre-scientific cultures with
strong mystical traditions. This did not mean that the system was mystical per se. It has taken us hundreds of years,
however, to separate these mental disciplines themselves
from the subject matter and the social context out of which
they evolved, to see that one's use of the systems was by
no means limited to the occult. It was perfectly safe to
use them in everyday life—even in the most mundane
and trite applications.

WHY SELECT THE READINGS RANDOMLY?

When first introduced to Mind Jogger, many people question
the value of random selection in choosing the readings.
"Why not just flip through the pages and read whatever
jumps out at you?" Or, "Why not just memorize every
reading in the book so that you can recall them whenever you wish?"

The advantage of random selection is that it bypasses old habits
of thinking. We tend to get stuck with problems because,
as one Mind Jogger enthusiast put it, "We keep looking
for the solutions in familiar but empty corners rather than
breaking out into new territories."

Why do we always look for answers in those familiar corners
that we already know will yield no answers? It is one of
life's ironies that when we're under pressure, as is often
the case when problems loom, we gravitate, frequently
against our will, toward the familiar and the promise of
"safety." That the familiar is empty or even painful seems
to matter less than the comfort of familiarity that it offers.
For most people, the survival reflex is to choose safety
first, knowledge and change second.

THE SECRETS OF THE SHAMAN

Carlos Castaneda tells the story of the shaman whose job it
was to provide a map of new hunting trails when game
was getting thin. His process was simple enough. He asked for a sheet of fresh rawhide which he laid out in the
sun to dry. After a few days passed, the hunters gathered
around the shaman and he directed a ceremonial dance
to the "prey gods."

After hours of dancing, the shaman of the hunt took out his
rawhide, crumpled it in his hands, said some prayers over
it, and then smoothed it out at the feet of the hunters.
The rawhide was now crisscrossed with lines and wrinkles.

▲

The shaman marked a few central reference points on the rawhide, and thus the new game map was created, with the wrinkles now representing the new trails the hunters should follow.

When the hunters followed the newly defined routes on the rawhide they nearly always discovered abundant game. Some say this system worked only because the hunters had exhausted the game on their previous hunting trails and thus **any** new path they followed would have yielded similar results.

There is a more important question to ask, one that has to do with human nature: If the maps were indeed random, why couldn't the hunters just tramp off into new territories on their own? What purpose did the shaman and his game map really serve? The answer to this is found more readily in modern psychology than in the ancient shaman traditions.

Humans tend to be creatures of habit. And those who are most skilled frequently are also the most dependent on habit. The baseball pitcher gets good at what he does by repeating the same movement again and again, until all the movements necessary for delivering the optimal pitch are etched in mind and muscle. Similarly, the musician is so practiced in sound, having fine-tuned his habits of listening, that he can easily detect a single sour note in a symphony. And so it is that the most skilled of us are frequently also the most bound to habit.

Random selection—be it for locating game trails or for solving problems—takes us out of our habitual ways of operating in the world. It forces us to look in the unfamiliar places. Were we to more consciously select our routes, we would be depending on the same habitual processes that got us stuck in the first place.

Though it is perhaps less earthy and colorful than the shaman's hunting map, Mind Jogger is at least as effective in the contemporary context for which it was designed. Instead

of rawhide baked in the sun, the Mind Jogger readings
and die will yield answers and solutions that will carry
you quite beyond everyday expectations.

In the following chapter I provide step by step instructions for
using Mind Jogger in a way that I have found to be both
creative and practical.

▲

GETTING ACQUAINTED

Flip through the readings, which begin on page 52, so that you
      can see how they are arranged and numbered.
You will note two things: First, each reading has two parts—
      the Text reading on one page, and the Guides on the next.
Each Text reading is only one paragraph long. However, the
      Guide page contains three separate parts, as follows:

SOURCE:
This Guide reading refers only to the **source** of your question or problem. You might look upon the Source reading
as guiding you toward an insight about the cause of the
problem you're working on: How did it begin, or what is
causing it to hang on?

OBSTRUCTION:
This Guide asks you to take a careful look at something
that is **standing in your way of clearly seeing the solution** to your question/problem. It may ask you to examine
something from which you must free yourself, or to consider a sacrifice you must make, in order for you to see
the solution to your present problem.

SOLUTION:
This Guide directs you to a solution.

THE FINE ART OF QUESTIONING

In every case, you begin by stating a question. The way you
      formulate your question for Mind Jogger can be as impor-
      tant as the subject matter itself. It is important to under-
      stand from the outset that when tension is high, as is char-
      acteristic of certain kinds of problems, it is usually difficult
      to find a positive way to describe the situation causing your
      tension. Instead, you may describe the frustration, anger,
      or confusion you're feeling. It can no doubt be valuable
      to express your negative feelings. But if those expressions

are mixed with your efforts to describe the problem clearly, these negative responses can easily prevent you from moving forward on the problem.

If you feel confused, angry, or frustrated at the moment you decide to turn to Mind Jogger for help, take a few moments to describe your negative or confused feelings before you do anything else. By doing this you discharge some of the negative feelings you are experiencing, thus allowing you to focus your attention on making a clear, positive statement about the problem. After writing down this "personal response" you will find that it takes much less effort to state your question or describe your problem.

Students of human behavior have demonstrated the fact, over and over again, that: "Negative statements tend to create walls against solution. Positive statements tend to create doors and windows."

Let's look at some specific ways of making positive statements that will lead you most directly to the solutions you're seeking.

RELAXATION EXERCISE

Your work with Mind Jogger is most productive when your mind is open and relaxed. Relax by doing the following before you state your problem:

Give yourself permission to take five or ten minutes to use Mind Jogger.

Sit back. Have both feet flat on the floor. If possible loosen any tight clothing. Have the palms of your hands open, resting on the tops of your thighs. Let your shoulders be loose and relaxed.

Open your mouth wide and yawn, or pretend you are yawning.

Let your mouth be loose. Let the areas around your eyes be loose. Let your forehead be loose.

If ideas or feelings come to your mind, urging you to think or act, pretend they are a ringing telephone that you observe but choose calmly not to answer. Truly important ideas or feelings will return when you are done with Mind Jogger. They will not be lost.

Take a deep breath. Hold it for a moment. Slowly exhale through your nose. Be aware of your chest relaxing.

Take a second deep breath. Hold it for a moment. Slowly exhale through your nose. Be aware of your abdomen rising.

Take a third deep breath. Hold it for a moment. Slowly exhale through your nose. Be aware of your lower body relaxing.

Take a fourth deep breath. Hold it for a moment. Slowly exhale through your nose. Be aware of your legs relaxing.

Now allow your breathing to return to normal.

Enjoy this relaxed and open state of mind.

▲

SOME QUESTIONS WORK BETTER THAN OTHERS

Here are some suggestions for stating problems for Mind Jogger:

The I-Action statement
Make an "I" statement that places you in the active role of seeking a solution. For example:

> "I want to know what I can do to solve the problem I am having with _____" (You fill in the blank, describing your problem.)

Keep It Positive
Spot negative words and rephrase your statement so that it is more positive. Practice this on one or two trial statements of your own and carefully note what happens. Especially observe the following:

Negative statements tend to be static, and they tend to anchor your thoughts and feelings in the negatives you describe.

Positive statements tend to be dynamic, and frequently suggest actions that you can take to alter the situation that is causing you trouble.

Positive statements nearly always motivate you to move forward to a solution. Here's an example:

By removing the negatives from his original statement that "Impossible conditions at work are making me miserable," one Mind Jogger user was motivated to reword his question as a possible action he could take: "I want to find a way to do my job so that it is enjoyable for me."

This understanding of positive and negative statements reveals the secret that makes "positive thinking" work as well as it does. In the final analysis, there is really no great mystery about the use of positive statements; it is simply the way the human mind responds to the structure of our language (a linear process): Negatives tend to keep our attention focused on moods or states of mind. Positives tend to start us thinking in terms of actions we can take to get out of those negative states of mind.

THE PROCEDURE SIMPLIFIED

Take a look at the Mind Jogger Sample Format, page 31–32. Each Mind Jogger consultation is done as I describe below. The process is the same whether you write your entries or not:

1. You begin by describing your personal reactions to a problem you are having. Be as elaborate as you wish here, expressing yourself freely.

2. State your "Question/Problem" in two lines or less. For best results state the problem or question in a positive way.

3. Cast the die to select your first reading. Note that each reading is separately numbered. Note also that each reading is two pages long. There is a Text reading, which is the first page of every reading. The second page of every reading contains the Guides that go with that Text. Turn to the Text reading indicated by the die. Study what it says, then turn the page and read only the reading entitled "Source." (Ignore the Obstruction and Solution readings.)

   Give yourself a few moments to think about what you've just read. Then ask yourself how the information you've just read applies to the problem or question you have brought to Mind Jogger.

4. Cast the die to select your second reading. This time, read the Text and the Obstruction readings. As before, ask yourself how the information presented in the Text and Obstruction readings apply to the problem or question you have brought to Mind Jogger.

▲

5. Cast the die for the third selection. Read the Text and only the Guide reading entitled "Solution." Then ask yourself how this information applies to the problem or question you have broght to Mind Jogger.

6. Take a moment to review what you've thought about so far and ask yourself what is the most important insight or discovery you've made.

7. Think about the work you have done thus far and decide on an action you can take to move toward a solution. (You will find that after reading the Texts and Guides that you will have an idea for a course of action you can take.) It is useful to break your action goals down into two parts:

Immediate Action: Although there is not always a long term goal for solving a problem, there is nearly always an immediate action that you can take. Examples: In deciding on whether or not to make a particular business trip, the most immediate action might be stated as: "Telephone travel agent and order airline tickets." The most immediate action for setting up a new business might be: "Schedule a meeting to talk over expansion plans with my business partner."

Long Term Goals: Not all questions or problems have long term goals, of course. For example, if you were making a choice between going on a business trip in the next four hours or staying at home, the Immediate Action statement would be most appropriate. On the other hand, if you had decided that you were going to start a new business in another city, you would definitely state that as a long term goal.

State long term goals and describe the immediate action you can take as briefly and precisely as you can.

MIND JOGGER SAMPLE FORMAT

1. Describe Your Personal Reactions To Your Present Problem
Or Question (Optional):

_____

_____

_____

2. State Your Question/Problem:

_____

_____

Readings:

3. First Selection:
Source:_____ # _____

How This Applies To Your Problem/Question:

_____

_____

_____

4. Second Selection:
Obstruction: _____ # _____

How This Applies To Your Problem/Question:

_____

_____

_____

5. Third Selection:
Solution: _____ # _____

How This Applies To Your Problem/Question:

_____

_____

_____

▲

6. Most Important Discovery?

_____

_____

7. The Most Immediate Action You Can Take:

_____

_____

A Long Term Goal:

_____

_____

For the complete Mind Jogger Journal, turn to page 94.

INTERPRETATIONS TELL IT ALL

In numbers three, four, and five, above, you recorded your inter-
        pretations of the readings. This is an extremely important
        part of the problem solving process presented here. How
        you do the interpretations will determine how useful
        Mind Jogger is to you. The formula for interpreting the
        readings is very simple. After studying a Mind Jogger
        reading you simply ask yourself, "How does this reading
        apply to the question/problem I am working on?" You
        then write down whatever comes to your mind.

The interpretation of the reading does two things: first, it allows
        you to integrate the ideas in the reading with your own
        thoughts and feelings, thus clarifying your own percep-
        tions for yourself; and second, it generates new ideas that
        have a clear sense of purpose and direction provided by
        both the Mind Jogger prompts and your own statement
        of the question/problem.

Because the interpretations are so valuable, you should take
your time with them. Write them down, and in the process
of working out the words that describe what you are thinking and feeling, you necessarily clarify and define issues,
making it possible to make decisions about what actions,
if any, you should take to resolve the stated problem.

EXAMPLE #1:

A young business woman concerned about a rumor that her
company would be announcing layoffs soon.

PROBLEM: There is a rumor that there are going to be some
layoffs at work. It's very hard to concentrate on work
with that hanging over our heads. I am about to quit and
start job junting, but my position here really is a good
one and I'd rather not let it go unless it's necessary.

QUESTION: What should I do about the situation at work—
stay where I am until I get more definite information
on layoffs, or start looking elsewhere?

FIRST SELECTION:

SOURCE: THE LULL
I see that I really am in a period when everything is sort
of stalled. What the reading means to me is that I should
take advantage of this time to think about my own career
directions. Nothing needs to be done right away.

SECOND SELECTION:

OBSTRUCTION: DARKNESS
Wow! I have been seeing only the dark side of the
layoff rumors, and putting all my attention into that.
But darkness can also be a time to rest for awhile, just
explore new things, new possibilities.

▲

THIRD SELECTION:

SOLUTION: EQUALIBRIUM

This is important to me right now, that I am really fighting it when I don't have to…change is occurring, and I should let it, instead of getting all excited and try to re-establish equalibirum. The change is going to be okay, and in the meantime I should take advantage of the lull to reassess what's going on in my life careerwise.

MOST IMPORTANT DISCOVERY: Even though I'm worried, I need to focus on where I am right now.

MOST IMMEDIATE ACTION: Here I'd have to say that I should take no action at all, that I should take a wait-and-see approach and in the meantime not fight it, using the time in a constructive way to think about my career decisions.

LONG TERM GOAL: The thing that comes to mind for me right now is that my long term goal is just to keep focused on my career, keeping my own progress forward-moving and focused, regardless of what happens with the companies I'm working for.

EXAMPLE #2:

A young father concerned about his young son's misbehavior in school.

PROBLEM: Mathew's teacher sent a note home saying that he has been talking back, "sassing" her, and wants us to do something about it. Mathew says the teacher was wrong…and from what he describes I'm inclined to agree.

QUESTION: I want to know how I should deal with this, so that we're not ignoring bad behavior if it is that, but so that we are supporting Mat if his story is right.

FIRST SELECTION:

SOURCE: STORM

Inner storms, the reading says. Could be Mat's trouble at school is a result of the problems he's having adjusting to his Debbie being away from the house more. He keeps complaining that Moms shouldn't go to school, only boys should.

SECOND SELECTION:

OBSTRUCTION: CHANGE

Change is normal but can cause distress...This seems right on with Mat. He needs to be encouraged to accept his mother going to school, that it is normal for mothers to do this. The more I think about it the more I see the trouble at school really is connected with what he's going through with the home situation.

THIRD SELECTION:

SOLUTION: TRADITION

Taking tradition in the broadest sense, the thing here is that in the past Mat and this teacher got along very well, and this problem did come up around the time his mom enrolled at school. We should pay attention to that, and try to remind him that he and his teacher used to be good friends.

MOST IMMEDIATE ACTION: Obviously, I know what has to be done, that is, talk to Mat about what he might be feeling—the inner storm idea—and assure him about that, and then tell him that he needs to clean up his act at school and get back to that place where he and his teacher were friends.

MOST IMPORTANT DISCOVERY: That Mat's having trouble with Debbie going to school.

LONG TERM GOALS: The thing that comes to mind here is keeping in touch with what's going on with Mat, so that he isn't carrying problems from home into school.

▲

EXAMPLE #3:

A young college woman who is having a disagreement
   with her fiance.

PROBLEM: Sometimes I think Kenneth is just an indecisive
   person. He doesn't want to make any kind of decision
   because it means commitment—where I am concerned,
   where his educational future is concerned, everything!
   I feel like he's pushing responsibility to make these
   decisions off on me, and I don't want it.

QUESTION: I want to know how to deal with Kenneth so
   that he makes his own decisions and doesn't get me
   to push on him to make them. When I do push on him
   we get into a huge fight and we both get stubborn
   and stomp off.

FIRST SELECTION:

SOURCE: HIGHER AUTHORITY
   A lot of ideas come up for me around this—first, that
   Ken is always looking for some authoritative answer,
   and most of the time there can't be such a thing. And I
   think he tries to make me into a kind of authority so
   he'll feel secure about his decision. Finally though, I
   see that I have to make my own voice clear to Ken,
   that I do not want to make his decisions for him. I
   really need to do that.

SECOND SELECTION:

OBSTRUCTION: PARADOX
   I guess there's a part of me that does like helping other
   people make decisions, but part of me that doesn't. For
   Ken and I to solve this problem we're having, I need to
   give up whatever it is I get from making decisions for
   other people. But I am going to. I know it is driving
   me crazy to have that kind of responsibility with him.

THIRD SELECTION:

SOLUTION: SPIRITUAL
>   At first I didn't see how this could be a spiritual thing,
>   but it is if you see that our relationship is going to be
>   in real trouble if we don't both get through this one.
>   I guess that is spiritual.

MOST IMPORTANT DISCOVERY: I need to stop making other
>   people's decisions for them.

MOST IMMEDIATE ACTION: When I think about the above,
>   it becomes so clear to me that I need to just tell Ken
>   everything I worked out above, and that I won't make
>   decisions for him any more. We both need to work out
>   our problems around this.

LONG TERM GOAL: is to watch myself about wanting to
>   help other people make decisions. I guess that's as
>   much of the problem between Ken and I as his not
>   wanting to make decisions. Come to think of it, he
>   does keep saying that.

▲

CHAPTER 3

WAYS TO APPLY MIND JOGGER

In the years that I have been working with Mind Jogger many
people have suggested ways to use it both professionally
and in their private lives. The suggestions have covered a
wide range of possibilities from the "Quickies" technique
described here to a technique which a nuclear physicist
described for his work which, not being a physicist, I un-
fortunately failed to understand. In this chapter I describe
what I feel are the most useful and universal applications.

I highly recommend keeping a journal of the work you do with
Mind Jogger since it allows you, over a period of time, to
keep track of goals you may set for yourself in the process
of working through a problem or question. If nothing
else, it is nice to have all your work in one place where
you can refer back to it for any reason.

QUICKIES

In the Table of Contents, you will find a list of the readings with
their corresponding numbers. After working with Mind Jogger for awhile you will find that you become quite familiar
with the general meaning of the readings. With that kind of
familiarity, you may find it useful to turn to the Index of
Readings and simply cast the die three times, noting the
name of the reading selected each time in the index.

When using Mind Jogger this way, you do not write down
your responses. Rather, you simply note the names of the
readings and ask yourself what they mean to you. This is
useful when you are stuck on a relatively simple problem
and want a gentle nudge to get you moving forward again.

DECISION MAKING

One of the most common uses of Mind Jogger is for decision
making. It is helpful in two ways: First, you can use it in
the beginning stages of collecting information upon
which to base an important decision. The method found
to be most effective in this is described below, under the

▲

heading of "Sharpening Creativity and Intuition—Access
To Your Hidden Resources." Second, it is useful in the final
stage, when you must make the decision itself.

Nine times out of ten, if you have done a thorough job of
collecting your information, the final stage of making the
decision will be clearcut. But it is that remaining one time
out of ten that gives you trouble—and that's where Mind
Jogger can be a godsend.

Decisions always involve change. And therein lies the key: If
you decide in favor of change, it usually means that you
or other people or both will have to make adjustments
in your lives, with all that this might imply. If you decide
against change, it usually means living with things as they
were—which is probably not completely satisfactory or the
issue of considering a change would never have arisen.

So decisions are nearly always **dichotomies,** that is, issues divided
between two points: in this case. (A) being in favor of
change, or (B) being in favor of things staying the same.

If you find yourself agonizing over the final stage of a decision,
or if you find yourself avoiding that final stage, there are
really only two possible questions to explore. Take out
Mind Jogger and state the problem in one of the two following ways (or both, if you wish to do two full readings): "I am in favor of this change and want to know
what I must do to move forward on that final decision."
Or, "I am in favor of things staying the same and want
to know what I must do to make that final decicion." If
you wish, you might be even more specific, stating that
you want help to understand what is making it difficult
for you to make the final decision.

Having asked the question continue the Mind Jogger reading
as described in the basic instructions, pages 29-30.

Because of the universal nature of decision making—that is,
decisions always involve a question of change—the process I describe here will work for virtually all decisions you
might face, either in your profession or in your private life.

BLOCK BUSTING

When the solution to **any** problem eludes you, using the same
methods that ordinarily work well for you, bear this in
mind: Sometimes the real problem lies in the **way** the
question is asked, not in the fact that there is no solution.
You may find that the particular way you are expressing
the problem is carrying you further and further from a
solution. The problem is becoming frustrating not because
there are no answers but because, as it is presently ex-
pressed, the question you are asking cannot yield the
solution you require.

How do we break such deadlocks? How do we "bust the
blocks?" The usual way is to step outside the boundaries
of the thought processes you are using at that moment.
There are a number of ways to do this, ranging from learning an entirely new set of problem-solving techniques to
talking the problem over with a friend or an expert who
can offer a broader perspective than you can presently
bring to bear. However, the prospect of learning an entirely new set of problem solving techniques when your
tolerance for frustration is already pushed to the limit is
seldom seen as a viable alternative. And the friend or expert who might help you is not always available when
you need them. That's when Mind Jogger can help.

At such a time, when you suspect that the question you are
asking is phrased in such a way that it can never yield a
solution, let Mind Jogger help you **step back** for a more
objective look. Instead of asking the most obvious question that comes to your mind, ask Mind Jogger questions
such as: "What is it about the way I am going about my
search for a solution that is blocking me from receiving
the answer I need?" Or, "I would like to discover a more
productive way to phrase my question."

Focus your work with Mind Jogger not directly on the problem
you are facing but on the questions you are asking as

▲

you search for solutions to that problem. Often, in the process of exploring the limits of your questions, solutions suddenly occur to you; when they don't, you will discover how to rephrase your questions so that they do yield the solutions you desire.

THE PERSONAL JOURNAL

For many years I have kept personal journals of my own Mind Jogger readings. There are a number of different ways to do this. Here are my own suggestions, along with suggestions made by others who are using Mind Jogger:

If I have a problem or question in my life I address the problem to Mind Jogger, as I described in the last chapter, and I record the work I do with it in my journal. Having this ongoing record is invaluable. As time passes I can look back and have a clear record of my progress on any issue that keeps coming up; if there isn't progress the written record often supplies clues for why there is not.

The perspective I have developed about my own ability to solve problems since I started recording my Mind Jogger readings in a journal has been very important to me. Two things happen: First, Mind Jogger provides a structure for solving problems, even the most mundane ones, that are ordinarily so elusive. Second, the ongoing record of the work I do with Mind Jogger in journal form provides me with concrete evidence of my ability to change the things that disturb me. I can look back over weeks or months or even years and see that I truly do have the power to solve problems and exert control over my life, bringing about changes that do bring me deep personal satisfaction.

Because most changes do occur in small increments, often spread out over many months or even years, they may sneak by us without notice. As a result we may never develop a sense of our own skills, our own power to shape our lives. To that end, the Mind Jogger diary is not unlike a photo album that, kept over a long period of time provides a record of changes—written "before and after" pictures that we wouldn't otherwise have. Where personal growth is concerned, this record can be an important affirmation of one's inner strengths and self-determination. (Mind Jogger Journal, page 94.)

UNDERSTANDING THE WISDOM OF DREAMS

In working with dreams, Mind Jogger can be an invaluable interpretive tool, which can be used separately or integrated with the journal described above. You simply present the dream as a question for Mind Jogger. For example, I recently had a dream in which I was on a canoe trip in Washington. Up ahead I could see heavy rapids, and the river was carrying me into a densely wooded area. I grew anxious. I considered going back upstream, but realized the current was too strong. At last I simply had to go with the current, and I did so with no mishaps.

I stated my question about this dream as follows: "I want to know what I can learn from this river and the situation in my dream." I cast the die and got the three following readings: Conflict, Communication, and Paradox. The conflict reading told me that a present discomfort I was feeling was the result of my struggle to transform an idea I had into a physical reality. I thought about how this related to my life. At the time I had begun to work on a book idea that seemed very risky for me, and I had been having difficulty maintaining a productive work schedule on it.

The idea for the book intrigued me but I had doubts that the manuscript had any commercial value whatsoever. If I were to continue working on the book I had to do so strictly as a selfish indulgence—at a time when I very much needed money to pay the bills. I was—like in the dream—being carried along a river into a **wilderness,** an **unknown territory,** and I could neither stop nor go back.

▲

The second reading, Communication, said that I should reevaluate my decision about how much I wanted to tell another person about my ideas. Where the book was concerned, I decided that I should not talk about my ideas to anyone else until I had finished at least a hundred pages. I cannot tell you how many times I have read this advice from other writers, that an author did himself a disservice by talking about a book that was still in progress. Doing so was dangerous for several reasons, the chief one being that telling your idea released you from the tension of wanting to finish your book or article. That tension is a great motivator in the lonely hours that are the writer's stock-in-trade.

The third reading, Paradox, told me to stop weighing pros and cons, that regardless of the choice I made about continuing work on the book, there would be paradoxes that I must accept. I took this to mean that I should, in effect, **go with the flow;** I should stop worrying about the commercial promise of the book idea I was working on, and should simply get on with it.

The most immediate action I thought I should take was to trust my idea and work on the manuscript at a comfortable pace, not allowing myself to yield to temptation and discuss my ideas with other people.   .

For a long term goal I stated simply, "Finish the book."

Through working on dreams with Mind Jogger, it has become clear to me that the interpretation of dreams as symbolic material is less productive than looking upon dreams as **experience.** Most brain researchers agree that where the subconscious mind is concerned there is no difference between imagined (or dreamed) experience, and the real thing. If this is so, the most useful "interpretation" of dreams would be to examine them in the same ways that we examine experiences in the real (i.e., physical) world.

In the dream example I gave above, "real" experience and "dream" experience were intertwined. In my real experi-

ences in canoes and float boats on rivers I had often
been fearful upon entering a rapids where I had never
been before, and I had learned that the safest and sometimes **only solution** was literally to go with the flow, putting
aside my fears in order to focus on the task of guiding the
boat through the current.

In my dream (above) I was not anticipating a river trip, so I asked
myself if there was any experience similar to this occurring
in my life, to which the same lessons might be applied.
That experience, it seemed to me, was the book project
which was carrying me along in spite of my fears. When
I applied the dream as a real life lesson it seemed to work
for me, that is, I was able to finish what I had started and
remain productive and creative in spite of the fears I was
experiencing.

Mind Jogger seems to be helpful in working with dreams
regardless of one's preference in the style of interpreting
them.

Although the following was suggested to me for use in a professional context, the same techniques can be applied
by the individual. It is an excellent "conflict resolution"
process whether for couples, co-workers, or friends.

COUPLES COUNSELING/CONFLICT RESOLUTION

Marriage counselors tell us that harmony in marriage comes
about not because the partners fully agree on every issue
but because they understand and can accept each other's
individual differences. That understanding and acceptance
is achieved only when each partner is able to clarify his
own thoughts and feelings and make them known to the
other person. Mind Jogger truly excels as a tool for helping
the partners in a marriage get to know each other better.

Here's how Barbara Peters, a marriage counselor in Michigan
uses Mind Jogger:

▲

"I have both parties sit down with pencil and paper and their
own copy of Mind Jogger. I then have them agree on a
single problem that they will work out. I tell them to stay
focused on their own thoughts and feelings about the
problem, rather than working on compromises or building
up an argument for their own position. At no time are
they to use the other person's name as they work the
problem through with Mind Jogger, nor are they to refer
to the other person in any way. The main purpose of this
is not to work out an immediate solution but to explore
one's own feelings on the matter.

"For example, a couple last week worked on a problem they
were having about sending their six year old daughter to
school. They both agreed to work on that issue—their
daughter's education. I had Tom, the husband, sit on one
side of the room, and Deborah, his wife, sit on the other.
I think this psychological distance is important.

"In about twenty minutes they had both worked through the
problem, including making a statement about an immediate
action and a long term goal they foresaw for solving the
issue. Then I had them exchange their Mind Jogger notes
and take fifteen minutes to carefully read the other person's comments. This done, I acted as a mediator while
they discussed their responses.

"With Deborah and Tom the results surprised us all. It turned
out that they were in complete agreement on a general
solution about the school issue. They both agreed that
they wanted their daughter to go to a private school—
though prior to that Deborah had mistakenly believed
that Tom wanted to keep their daughter in public school.
The conflict had arisen because their general philosophies
about education were quite different. After looking carefully at what the other person really thought and felt they
were able to respect each others' philosophical differences
because regardless of those differences they agreed on
the course of action they would take."

No subject in marriage is beyond the scope of Mind Jogger.
Be it sex, money, or who does the dishes, Mind Jogger
will help you clarify your own thoughts, feelings, and
goals, and will provide you with a structured format for
sharing these findings with your mate (and vice versa).
Here is a step-by-step description of the process I've described
in the example above:
Step One: The mates choose a single problem they will ask
Mind Jogger.
Step Two: Both people sit down and work this problem through
with Mind Jogger, in relative privacy. They focus on their
own thoughts and feelings and do not in any way refer
to the other person in their notes.
Step Three: The mates then exchange their work and study
what the other had to say.
Step Four: The two then discuss the problem in light of the
new information revealed in the work with Mind Jogger.
This same process can be used in working out conflicts in the
work environment.

SHARPENING CREATIVITY AND INTUITION—
ACCESS TO YOUR HIDDEN RESOURCES

We each have within us vast warehouses of knowledge that
ordinarily lie just beyond the reach of our everyday methods
—such as math, logic, or whatever other methods we
use for figuring out solutions to the problems we face
in our jobs and personal lives. The knowledge we don't
access with our everyday methods is often referred to as
"intuition" or "creativity" or "inner knowledge" or "hidden resources." Everyone has this inner knowledge and
most people make use of it from time to time. But most
people also believe that they can tap into it only seren-
dipitously—in times of crisis, or in unguarded moments
when they are unaware of the methods they are using
to do this. It does not occur to them that they might

▲

develop skills that can provide them access to these
vast warehouses any time they wish.

Mind Jogger provides a specific mental tool, a structured
method for utilizing our inner knowledge at will.

The method is simple.

Step One: Instead of beginning your work with Mind Jogger in
the usual way, that is, by stating your problem, state instead that you want to gain access to everything you
know about a particular subject. For example, a physician
who used it in this way asked, "I want to gain access to
everything I know about spinal injuries. (A problem suf-
fered by one of his patients, which was not responding
to standard treatment)."

Take notes, but do not write in great detail. Detailed or pon-
derous notes put you in a left brain mode, which we
want to avoid. To stay as much as possible in the right
brain mode, while still keeping a record of what you're
doing, try drawing sketches or symbols of your ideas, or
jot down two or three line reminders that you can go
back to later. Some people use a tape recorder for this—
which I encourage because recording your voice requires
somewhat less left-brain participation than writing.

Step Two: Make as many casts of the die as you wish. But read
only the overall readings, not the source, obstruction,
or solution readings.

Step Three: On each cast, go further than reading the words:
Let your mind, as one person said, "wrap around" the
ideas. As you become engaged with the ideas you are, in
fact, bringing your inner resources into focus.

Step Five: Look over the ideas you have recorded. You will find
that some apply to the original problem or question you
asked while others do not. Understand that the ideas you
came up with are from your own warehouses or inner
knowledge, and that your work with Mind Jogger was
what brought you to the door where you could enter
and retrieve what you needed.

PSYCHIC WORK AND MIND JOGGER

Mind Jogger can be applied in psychic work and is as useful for the learner as it is for the advanced reader. The following instructions will be helpful in either case, though for the beginner I do recommend working with a reputable teacher.

When preparing to do a psychic reading, the psychic begins by putting him/herself in a receptive state of mind. For most people this is a quiet state, one in which there is no internal "noise" or interference, a state of mind in which the person is free of the distractions of his or her own thoughts. Meditation techniques are ordinarily named as the first step. However, many people have difficulty clearing their own thoughts enough even to start the physical relaxation necessary for meditation. Mind Jogger is invaluable for that, providing a conscious structure for a process that many psychics do unconsciously.

Step One: Instead of describing a problem or question, you start your work with Mind Jogger by stating "I want to know what I must do to get into a quiet and receptive state of mind."

Step Two: Cast the die and select three readings, following the standard Mind Jogger process described on pages 25 to 32. **Do not write down your responses, and do not get into any questions about Immediate Actions and Long Term Goals.**

Put the Mind Jogger aside and be in a relaxed position, lying down or sitting in a comfortable chair or resting in a favorite Yoga posture.

Step Three: Allow yourself to be aware of thoughts and feelings that come up for you following your work with Mind Jogger, as described above. But give yourself permission to do nothing about these thoughts and feelings other than to acknowledge their presence.

Imagine that you are lying on your back in a warm and comfortable place, perhaps the beach, perhaps in an open

▲

meadow, perhaps in the mountains—wherever you feel comfortable, alive, joyous, safe, receptive.

Imagine that the thoughts and feelings that come to your mind are like birds passing overhead, passing into your field of vision, perhaps circling for a moment, and then flying away. Understand that all thoughts and feelings have lives of their own, and there is nothing you need do at this moment to feed them, nurture them, or follow them. Let them go.

Take a deep breath. Hold it for a moment. Exhale slowly through your nose. Do this three or four times, and as you do, notice how your body is relaxing.

If you feel tense in any part of your body, imagine that part relaxing as you take a deep breath and then exhale slowly through your nose.

You will feel deeply relaxed now. Your mind is at ease. Every muscle in your body feels soft, warm, pleasantly energetic.

Your mind is open, free to receive information about your own life or a client's life or the life of a loved one.

Now, in this same relaxed, open state of mind, ask a question that you or the other person wants answered.

(If you wish to make a record of your reading at this point, use a tape recorder. Writing is linear and will take you out of the receptive state of mind.)

You may ask the question aloud or ask it only in your mind.

Cast the die and read only the Text reading of that selection. Sit quietly with that reading for a moment.

Now think about the question you wanted psychically answered. Simply receive whatever comes in, without making any effort to ask how it applies to either the Mind Jogger Text you've just read or the question you wish to answer.

(Think of the Mind Jogger Text readings only as "prompts," for you, "priming the psychic pump," as one person put it.)

For best results, speak aloud to record whatever you receive on the tape recorder. Don't depend on your memory to recall readings of this kind.

You may go through as many Mind Jogger selections as you
   wish. If some selections do not seem to bring up anything
   for you, ignore them and select others. If a single reading
   prompts you sufficiently, don't feel that you have to make
   another. Sometimes a single reading opens exactly the
   channel you need.

When you feel that you want to stop, say aloud "I am going
   to stop now," or use similar words that give you a sense
   of completion and closure.

If you are with another person—especially if you have been
   doing a reading for them—reach out and take their hand,
   giving it a squeeze. This puts you in contact with the
   every day world.

Frequently, when doing psychic readings, the person for whom
   you are reading will also get into a deeply relaxed, open,
   and vulnerable state of mind. And it is important for that
   person, as well as for you, to leave that relaxed and open
   state of mind, and come back to your everyday state of
   mind in order to carry out your everyday responsibilities.

Finally, go back to the closing structure of Mind Jogger and
   ask what Immediate Action you or the other person may
   wish to take in view of the reading you have made.
   Then, if applicable, also set a Long Term Goal.

The immediate action and goal setting process provides a solid
   closure to a reading, and this "grounding" is important
   since it brings the information back into the context of
   the everyday world.

▲

CHAPTER 4

THE READINGS

Texts & Guides

1

TRADITION

Traditional values may endure not out of habit or fear of change but because they offer something of value. However, rigidly following tradition in the form of laws, language, or social ethics may blind us to more satisfying and appropriate alternatives. One's ignorance of tradition may result in repeating the same errors others before us have made.

Guide 1

SOURCE:
Fear of a new path may prevent
you or someone close to you from
finding solutions to a present problem. Your knowledge of the accepted path is valuable in evaluat-
ing new possibilities.

OBSTRUCTION:
Give up the false security of an
accepted path. At the same time
take heed of what others before
you have done. Learn from other's
errors.

SOLUTION:
Study the past and you will
discover new knowledge. Alternatives will become clear when
you acknowledge tradition and
forge new paths that avoid errors
which others have already made.

▲

2

PARADOX

To care about anything makes us vulnerable to both pleasure and pain: Those who dare to love must risk the pain of losing that love. Those who strive to achieve material wealth must risk losing that wealth. There is comfort in knowledge but with that knowledge comes the burden of awareness. Fame means enjoying recognition, on one hand, the loss of privacy on the other. No important experience is without its paradox. Likewise, paradox respects no socio-economic boundaries; it is as prevalent in failure as in success.

Guide 2

SOURCE:
Your present problem has arisen
because you have misinterpreted a
paradox. An undesirable outcome,
as the result of an action you took,
is not a sign of a wrong decision.

OBSTRUCTION:
Accept both positive and negative
sides of a recent decision or action.
Let go of something valued, risk
loss even though you may suffer
others' judgements. There is no
other way to reach your goal.

SOLUTION:
Stop weighing pros and cons. There
will be a paradox regardless of the
choice you make. Personal power
comes with your acceptance of the
paradox and your commitment to
action.

▲

3

THE LULL

Lulls follow periods of intense activity. These can be perceived as restful, boring, anxiety-producing, or even depressing. They may be used as opportunities to recoup or viewed as times of deprivation, loss and foreboding. Highly productive people may feel a sense of loss or even a sense of fear or negativity about the future during lulls. A lull may also be the goal of a person who seeks and enjoys leisure. The lull is an essential life rhythm like the rest between heartbeats. Learn to see all lulls as valleys in a broad landscape whose hills, forests, highways, deserts, and skyscapes are forever unfolding. Your choices in the ways you may interpret lulls are unlimited.

Guide 3

SOURCE:
You may feel that nothing is moving forward, that you are making
no progress toward your realization
of an important goal. The problem
is not that you are not making progress —on the contrary, the lull is
a healthy part of an important
progression.

OBSTRUCTION:
This is a time to do nothing.
Acknowledge the lull as an integral
part of a much larger cycle of progress. You will understand the solution to your present problem only
when you relinquish the impulse
to find a reason for the lull.

SOLUTION:
The solution to your present problem will come to you when you
least expect it. You need no longer
push or make great efforts to find
what you are seeking. Consider
the lull useful to you now.

▲

Text

4

CHANGE

Change can be large or small, gentle or wrenching. When one senses that it is inevitable, emotions run high—from optimism and invigoration, to foreboding and loss of energy. Even change for the better can trigger profound feelings of loss, since even positive change usually requires letting go of something secure or familiar. Fear of loss—letting go of the familiar, even when it is uncomfortable—can be so great that it discourages healthy or necessary change. We have the power to accept or reject feelings that signal us to change but by doing so we frequently experience greater discomfort.

Guide 4

SOURCE:
You are presently working very
hard to overcome a major resistance to change. This resistance
may be your own or someone
else's. You have invested a great
deal of time and energy in the
change that is about to occur, and
you need to take care that you
don't get in your own way now.

OBSTRUCTION:
Make room for change by letting
go of something familiar and
known. You will begin to see the
solution to your present problem
when you understand that the
discomfort of changing is now
less than the discomfort of staying
the same.

SOLUTION:
The discomfort you presently feel
will pass as you let go of something familiar and allow an important change to occur. Recognize
that you have participated, perhaps
without knowing it, in bringing
about this change. You will ultimately benefit.

5

PROJECTION

We each create our own world. This is not to say that there is no "real" world out there. Rather, we perceive reality through a two-step process: First, we recognize the existence of the outside "world" through sensory impressions that in and of themselves have no substance or meaning. Second, we assign meaning to these sensory impressions on the basis of what we know and feel at that moment. These constitute our "projections," interpretations of reality that are more or less accurate but are never **exactly like reality.** As you recognize and accept the fact that you live in a world of your own projections you begin to enjoy the simple luxuries of humor and patience and love. It becomes clear that your own judgements are the closest you can ever come to truth and such truths confirm the importance of trusting and supporting yourself in your own life. Your thoughts and actions are the vehicles that carry you to success.

Guide 5

SOURCE:
The present problem has arisen
because of the disparity between
the "real" world and the projections of people involved—including
you. The conflicting points of view
reveal the true identities of the people involved. The issue is not to
uncover the truth but to understand those people better by looking closely at the nature of their
projections.

OBSTRUCTION:
Relinquish your present search for
"rightness," or justice, viewing the
problem or question first as a way
of revealing the identities of the
people involved and only after that
as an issue of justice or rightness.

SOLUTION:
Focus all your attention on your
projection, not on discovering
some absolute truth about the
external world. The only important
truth to be discovered in the present question/problem is the nature
of your projection. There is nothing
else.

▲

Text

6

SELF-COMMUNICATION

We each possess a vast warehouse of information about the world, collected not just through formal education but through first-hand experiences, stories we have been told, things we have imagined and memories that are carried genetically. You possess more information about yourself than anyone else in the world can ever have about you. When self-communication is developed and encouraged, you become your own expert about what is right for you. This is especially important when making personal choices since only through self-communication can you gain access to that warehouse of self-knowledge which only you possess. Self-communication is the only path to intuition.

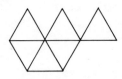

Guide 6

SOURCE:
You have been neglecting self-communication. You have sought answers to a present problem in sources outside yourself, not realizing that the knowledge you require is private, your own possession.

OBSTRUCTION:
You will begin to see your solution as you give up your belief that the answer you require can be found in other people. You already possess the knowledge you need.

SOLUTION:
Recognize the richness of your own knowledge, including, but not limited to, your formal learning: Seek new forms of self-communication to open new channels to your valuable inner resources.

7
CONFLICT

All human conflicts, as well as achievements, begin as ideas. Ideas become realities only when people believe in them so strongly that they would risk their own physical or mental comfort to act on them. There is great strength in complete commitment to an idea or belief. There is also potential for great conflict. The more personal risk you take the more you may feel resistance or opposition. This is especially true if you are opposed by a person whose commitment to his or her idea is as powerful as your own. If you know the other person is willing to risk as much as you, your body signals you to defend yourself just as it would with a physical threat. Recognize that strong physical responses are also good measures of the strength of your commitment to an idea or belief.

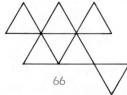

Guide 7

SOURCE:
Distress that you feel in a present
conflict is making itself known as
physical discomfort or even disease.
The source of this discomfort is
your struggle to make an idea into
a physical reality. Explore your own
level of commitment.

OBSTRUCTION:
The solution to your present problem will come as you temporarily
suspend your desire to achieve
harmony. An important idea is at
stake. Have courage as you face
a conflict and you will gain valuable
knowledge about yourself.

SOLUTION:
By exercising your courage to confront a person who is opposing
you, you will find deep understanding of him or her. Or the confrontation will result in separation,
with increased respect for the importance of acknowledging human
differences.

▲

Text

8

NEGOTIATION

Satisfactory solutions to conflicts with important associates or friends come about now only through open negotiation. Conflicts that result in one person subverting another person's needs never stay settled. Both parties—the one doing the subverting as well as the person subverted—must share responsibility for the failure of such "solutions." Longer lasting solutions that respect all persons who are involved require great patience to bring about. But these agreements can be maintained comfortably and will ultimately profit everyone.

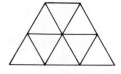

Guide 8

SOURCE:
Compromises made in the past—
either formally or by default—are
the source of present fears or
resentments. That past compromise
must be re-negotiated.

OBSTRUCTION:
Relinquish the idea that one person
must give up his or her needs to
satisfy the other. There is no absolute way to determine "right"
or "wrong" in this problem. Work
for equality.

SOLUTION:
Express your own needs in the present problem but realize that your
long-term interests will be served
only if you are careful to study the
needs of the other person involved.
Give joint interests equal consid-
eration.

9

COMMUNICATION

The expression of ideas and feelings allows others to know our needs and expectations. These exchanges can have both positive and negative effects: For example, the effective leader communicates a plan of action but does not reveal personal doubts about the potential outcome of that plan, since those doubts can undermine other people's efforts to carry the plan forward to success. Similarly, the impulse always to communicate the truth can mask the desire to use that truth to injure the person with whom they are communicating.

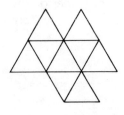

Guide 9

SOURCE:
To get to the roots of the present
problem focus on your efforts to
communicate an important piece of
information to another person or
persons. Your reasons for doing
so are not as they appear on the
surface.

OBSTRUCTION:
Re-evaluate your decision about
how much or how little you should
communicate your ideas or feelings
to another person(s).

SOLUTION:
The solution to your problem will
be found in a new understanding
of a responsibility connected with
your communication of important
information to another person.

10
PERSONAL POWER

Personal power is the ability to know yourself and use your personal resources and assets in ways that will bring you, as well as others, maximum benefits. It is the power to utilize your own knowledge, experience and intuition for creating objects, relationships, new ideas, businesses, physical structures, etc., that are truly an expression of you. It is the source of your strength in making decisions that will truly serve and benefit you, rather than only gaining you the approval of others. Those who are most successful trust their personal power but also understand that inner resources are constantly renewed by listening to what others have to offer. Self power can turn into loneliness and disappointment if **listening** is neglected.

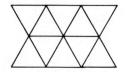

Guide 10

SOURCE:
Your present problem once more
exhibits your need to establish a
more satisfactory balance between
your personal power and your
interdependence with other people.

OBSTRUCTION:
Give up the belief that your power
lies only in establishing alliances
with other people. They cannot
give you **power.** They can provide
valuable nutriment but only when
you see and respect your own
inner resources.

SOLUTION:
Embrace your inner resources. Be
fully supportive of what is truly
you. Doing this is the foundation for
all true and secure personal power.
Listen to other people but don't
mistake their power as your own.

11
PATIENCE

Patience is the key to successful and productive self-discipline. You achieve what you desire not by **imposing your will** over the way you spend your time but by embracing your beliefs, your passions and your dedication to a larger plan. To achieve the goals of a larger plan you make choices about the way to spend time or money in the present, sacrificing immediate gratification for the satisfaction of the larger plan. When the balance is right, there is no sense of deprivation, since you are working in the service of your own greatest interests. Then, when the larger goal is finally achieved the habit of patience must give way to the enjoyment of that personal achievement.

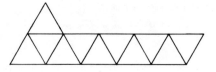

Guide 11

SOURCE:
The tension you now experience
is the result of questioning whether
the achievement of your larger
goals will pay off in rewards that
are worth your sacrifice.

OBSTRUCTION:
To achieve your goal, stand back
and carefully look at ways you
presently use your personal resources. Look at sacrifices that
have become deprivations; those
which are not in some way satisfying are obstructions and should
be changed.

SOLUTION:
Look long and hard at an important goal. Evaluate the probability
of your success and decide if you
need to change the ways you are
presently using your resources. You
may need to increase, decrease or
in some other way change your
commitments.

12
FLEXIBILITY

We are all affected by beliefs and feelings—which ultimately are the source of all personal motivation. These are the cornerstones upon which we build our lives. When our thoughts and feelings are challenged, it can seem as though our very lives are in danger. The ability to let go of the thoughts and feelings that direct our lives can open doors to new knowledge and new experience. It is important to know that suspending one's thoughts and feelings briefly does not negate them forever; they will return. Look upon the **willing suspension of belief** as a personal choice, creating space for other voices, other knowledge to be heard. We grow by receiving what others have to give, not by constructing shields that make even our physical bodies inflexible.

Guide 12

SOURCE:
The key to understanding the present problem is found in one person
being too flexible while another
too rigidly clings to his/her point of
view. One person is taking responsibility for another, creating tension
and resentment that are being
masked.

OBSTRUCTION:
Temporarily suspend important feelings and long-held personal beliefs.
This suspension opens wide the
door for change, which is now re-
quired if you wish to move forward.

SOLUTION:
Learn to suspend your most strongly
held beliefs so that new information can come in and new relationships can develop. At the same
time, define the lines between your
flexibility and your submission to
others.

13
EQUALIBRIUM

The impulse to maintain equalibrium or balance is constant throughout nature. Change is also constant, and while change is occurring there may be an illusion that equalibrium is lost. Fighting to achieve equalibrium at such times is counterproductive, and can lead to chaos. All life is cyclic, rising and falling, getting better, getting worse, getting better again. Mankind's search for equalibrium can be noble; just as often it can be destructive. Thus, relinquishing the impulse to regain or maintain equalibrium may be a sign of strength and wisdom.

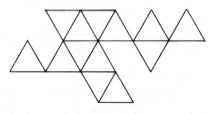

Guide 13

SOURCE:
Things are not out of balance. The
real problem is in the perception of
imbalance—yours or another person's—resulting in an unnecessary
struggle to fix something that
doesn't need to be fixed. This effort
is preventing necessary change.

OBSTRUCTION:
Give up, or help others to give up, a
struggle to maintain an old system,
routine, or belief system. Trust that
the resulting change will bring many
benefits for all.

SOLUTION:
The solution to the problem you
are facing lies not in maintaining or
restoring equalibrium but in allowing change to occur.

14
CREATIVITY

The ability to manipulate ideas, objects, materials, experiences, and even relationships with people, is essential for living a successful and productive life. Such creativity is a powerful use of your personal resources. But even though creativity is usually positive, it can also be destructive since through it you can invent problems where previously there were none.

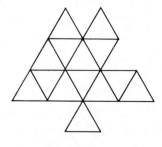

Guide 14

SOURCE:
Look at both the positive and negative aspects of creativity in the
present problem; along with the
creation of solutions you may find
that problems are being created
unnecessarily.

OBSTRUCTION:
Something that you once created,
and which served a useful purpose,
is now working against you. Relinquish your attachment to this past
creation and you will see new
solutions.

SOLUTION:
Look carefully at a personal creation that once made an important
contribution in your life; it is now
at the center of a problem. Relinquish that creation and move
forward.

INTUITION

Intuituion is knowledge that we each have within us but which we may not be fully aware that we possess. Often intuition is knowledge that comes from sources other than books, teachers, consultants, our superiors, etc. Such knowledge may prove more valuable than the knowledge that authorities and would-be experts offer. Intuition is partly congenital, partly what we have acquired through experience. It is dependable and ultimately the most important source of knowledge we can turn to in choosing careers, mates, places to live, etc. To be strongly intuitive means to be in touch with one's greatest personal convictions, able to gain access to one's personal resources easily and quickly.

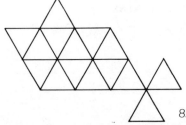

Guide 15

SOURCE:
In the problem you presently face
there is a struggle between trusting
your intuition and turning to experts
or other authorities. That is the root
of the problem.

OBSTRUCTION:
Give up the hope that experts or
authorities will relieve you of the
burden of making an important
choice in your life. Your own
intuition holds all the answers
you require.

SOLUTION:
Collect whatever information you
can, then stop analyzing. Relax
and allow your own intuition
to dictate your final choice.

16

SPIRITUAL

No matter how far science, psychology, technology, art, or industry take us, there continue to be unknowns or experiences that cannot be explained in simple linear terms. These are usually what we term "spiritual" concerns. We all have experiences in this realm, whether they be found in our awe of the infinite complexity of the universe itself or with our faith in a personal God. In addition, there are human needs and interactions that have spiritual implications—the need for self-esteem, for a sense of our own power, the need to love and be loved, the support and strength of family bonds, or faith in our serving a purpose larger than ourselves. These exert powerful influences in our lives and can be understood only as spiritual values.

Guide 16

SOURCE:
Spiritual values and needs in your
life are being overshadowed because
you feel you must focus your attention on other priorities—i.e. business, scientific, technological, etc.

OBSTRUCTION:
The present problem may seem
obvious, but its total solution is
discovered only by putting aside
scientific, technological or other
systematic processes, to look at
broadly spiritual concerns.

SOLUTION:
A solution to your problem lies outside physical, intellectual, or emo-
tional realms. These are important
but final resolution that can only be
found by including the spiritual.

17

HIGHER
AUTHORITY

The lifespan of each person is miniscule compared to the life of the planet or the universe. Personal knowledge counts for little within this scheme of things—yet it counts for much within our own lives. Awed by our little-ness, we seek support from higher authorities, or from groups. Sometimes, even as we seek this support, such associations can diminish or undermine the importance of personal power. The balance between self-trust and trust in a higher authority is always in flux. This balance should always be considered whenever personal power and self-esteem are threatened or low.

Guide 17

SOURCE:
There is an imbalance between
your self-power and the power
you have relinquished to a higher
authority. Your personal voice is not
clear at this moment and this is
causing problems for you as well
as others.

OBSTRUCTION:
The evidence that you have collected for making an important
decision is **incomplete** though **not
wrong** in the ordinary sense.
Examine an imbalance between
your own knowledge and that of
a higher or "other" authority, and
be prepared to give up your depen-
dency on authority in order to
achieve a personal need.

SOLUTION:
Gather information to find a solution to your present problem by
seeking others' counsel or expertise. But honor the fact that the
final decision is yours alone.

▲

18
INNOCENCE

Before you have experienced a thing first hand, your thoughts and feelings about it are abstract and untested. Such abstractions may help prepare you for the real thing, or they may distort your understanding of it, leading to wide confusion and faulty judgements. Real experience tests the abstraction, pitting it against the checks and balances of your senses, your knowledge, and your feelings. The solid knowledge you gain from confrontation with reality provides information that often becomes the source of great personal strength. Judgements made from knowledge gained by first hand experience are much more likely to yield the desired results than judgements made through abstraction.

Guide 18

SOURCE:
There are many ways to look at
your present problem. You now see
only one way of looking—and in
this way your abstractions are preventing you from seeing the most
important issues.

OBSTRUCTION:
Face a fear that is now preventing
you from directly experiencing
something related to the present
problem. The solution becomes
clear only when you dissolve the
abstraction by leaving your inno-
cence behind.

SOLUTION:
You have been attempting to solve
a problem by applying information
that you have not experienced first
hand. This is distorting the real
issues. Dissolve the abstraction
with firsthand experience.

19
DARKNESS

Darkness is commonly perceived as negative. It symbolizes the unseen or even the "forbidden fruits." However, writers since the beginning of time have seen darkness as the source of constructive experience and knowledge. In the Book of Job, we are told "He discovereth deep things out of darkness." Similarly, though the term "dark inner self" connotes something potentially evil, that part of the self is more positive than negative. We sometimes use the darkness as a way of avoiding action: for example, by looking only at our failures in life and convincing ourselves that we can't possibly succeed in a present venture. But by looking more deeply into the darkness, we see past our own disappointments and fears and discover the best in ourselves.

Guide 19

SOURCE:
You are seeing only darkness and
negativity in a present problem.
The darkness is there but you have
yet to discover the positive resources that are present within it.

OBSTRUCTION:
As you cease to cling to your own
fears about the darkness which
you associate with the present
problem, you will discover that
the darkness masks very positive
resources.

SOLUTION:
You already know the solution to
the present problem. But you will
become fully aware of that solution
only as you give up the negative
illusions that you are projecting to
the darkness.

THE STORM

In the natural world storms destroy man-made structures. In our inner world, storms of a different kind bring turmoil, challenging thoughts and feelings, and even destroying once highly valued personal points of view. Even so, inner storms, in and of themselves, are neither positive nor negative. An old structure destroyed makes room for the new, which might be more refined, richer in content, more complex, larger, etc. A storm might also leave an empty space in which to create something entirely new. Storms on the horizon only mean change in the making. After the storm passes, there is usually no choice but to accept the changes it brought. There is, however, a choice about how to interpret and make use of the change.

Guide 20

SOURCE:
Tension, anxiety, or restlessness
that you are presently experiencing
is the product of an inner storm.
The discomfort is caused not by the
storm's threat but by your own
natural reflexes to resist changes
produced by the storm.

OBSTRUCTION:
As an inner storm passes, give yourself time to mourn the loss of important beliefs, feelings, a place, or even
a person you have lost. Accept the
loss of an old way. Let go.

SOLUTION:
Important beliefs, feelings or relationships have been destroyed by
an inner storm. Mourn the loss,
then watch for the clearing where
something new will grow.

▲

CHAPTER 5
MIND JOGGER
JOURNAL

This section is included so that you can create a permanent
record of your work with Mind Jogger. It will prove to be
particularly valuable for creating your own Personal Journal, as described in Chapter Three. Once you have filled
in these pages they become a valuable reference, reminding you of themes, inner strengths, and recurring issues
that are integral to your life—specific inner resources that
you bring to every challenge you confront in your life.
You will find more about the use of this journal on pages
38 to 51.

▲

DATE: _____

PROBLEM: _____

_____

_____

QUESTION: _____

_____

_____

FIRST SELECTION: SOURCE _____

_____

_____

_____

_____

SECOND SELECTION: OBSTRUCTION _____

_____

_____

_____

_____

THIRD SELECTION: SOLUTION _____

_____

_____

_____

_____

M I N D   J O G G E R

MOST IMPORTANT DISCOVERY: _____

_____

_____

_____

_____

_____

MOST IMMEDIATE ACTION: _____

_____

_____

_____

_____

_____

LONG TERM GOAL: _____

_____

_____

_____

_____

_____

NOTES: _____

_____

_____

_____

▲

DATE: _____

PROBLEM: _____

_____

_____

QUESTION: _____

_____

_____

FIRST SELECTION: SOURCE _____

_____

_____

_____

_____

SECOND SELECTION: OBSTRUCTION _____

_____

_____

_____

_____

THIRD SELECTION: SOLUTION _____

_____

_____

_____

_____

M I N D   J O G G E R

MOST IMPORTANT DISCOVERY: _____

_____

_____

_____

_____

_____

MOST IMMEDIATE ACTION: _____

_____

_____

_____

_____

_____

LONG TERM GOAL: _____

_____

_____

_____

_____

_____

NOTES: _____

_____

_____

_____

▲

DATE: _____

PROBLEM: _____

_____

_____

QUESTION: _____

_____

_____

FIRST SELECTION: SOURCE _____

_____

_____

_____

_____

SECOND SELECTION: OBSTRUCTION _____

_____

_____

_____

_____

THIRD SELECTION: SOLUTION _____

_____

_____

_____

_____

M I N D   J O G G E R

MOST IMPORTANT DISCOVERY: _____

_____

_____

_____

_____

_____

MOST IMMEDIATE ACTION: _____

_____

_____

_____

_____

_____

LONG TERM GOAL: _____

_____

_____

_____

_____

_____

NOTES: _____

_____

_____

_____

▲

DATE: _____

PROBLEM: _____

_____

_____

QUESTION: _____

_____

_____

FIRST SELECTION: SOURCE _____

_____

_____

_____

_____

SECOND SELECTION: OBSTRUCTION _____

_____

_____

_____

_____

THIRD SELECTION: SOLUTION _____

_____

_____

_____

_____

M I N D   J O G G E R

MOST IMPORTANT DISCOVERY: _____

_____

_____

_____

_____

_____

MOST IMMEDIATE ACTION: _____

_____

_____

_____

_____

_____

LONG TERM GOAL: _____

_____

_____

_____

_____

_____

NOTES: _____

_____

_____

_____

▲

DATE: _____

PROBLEM: _____

_____

_____

QUESTION: _____

_____

_____

FIRST SELECTION: SOURCE _____

_____

_____

_____

_____

SECOND SELECTION: OBSTRUCTION _____

_____

_____

_____

_____

THIRD SELECTION: SOLUTION _____

_____

_____

_____

_____

M I N D   J O G G E R

MOST IMPORTANT DISCOVERY: _____

_____

_____

_____

_____

MOST IMMEDIATE ACTION: _____

_____

_____

_____

_____

LONG TERM GOAL: _____

_____

_____

_____

_____

NOTES: _____

_____

_____

_____

▲

DATE: _____

PROBLEM: _____

_____

_____

QUESTION: _____

_____

_____

FIRST SELECTION: SOURCE _____

_____

_____

_____

_____

SECOND SELECTION: OBSTRUCTION _____

_____

_____

_____

_____

THIRD SELECTION: SOLUTION _____

_____

_____

_____

_____

106

M I N D J O G G E R

MOST IMPORTANT DISCOVERY: _____

_____

_____

_____

_____

_____

MOST IMMEDIATE ACTION: _____

_____

_____

_____

_____

_____

LONG TERM GOAL: _____

_____

_____

_____

_____

_____

NOTES: _____

_____

_____

_____

▲

DATE: _____

PROBLEM: _____

_____

_____

QUESTION: _____

_____

_____

FIRST SELECTION: SOURCE _____

_____

_____

_____

_____

SECOND SELECTION: OBSTRUCTION _____

_____

_____

_____

_____

THIRD SELECTION: SOLUTION _____

_____

_____

_____

_____

M I N D   J O G G E R

MOST IMPORTANT DISCOVERY: _____

_____

_____

_____

_____

_____

MOST IMMEDIATE ACTION: _____

_____

_____

_____

_____

_____

LONG TERM GOAL: _____

_____

_____

_____

_____

_____

NOTES: _____

_____

_____

_____

▲

DATE: _____

PROBLEM: _____

_____

_____

QUESTION: _____

_____

_____

FIRST SELECTION: SOURCE _____

_____

_____

_____

_____

SECOND SELECTION: OBSTRUCTION _____

_____

_____

_____

_____

THIRD SELECTION: SOLUTION _____

_____

_____

_____

_____

M I N D   J O G G E R

MOST IMPORTANT DISCOVERY: _____

_____

_____

_____

_____

_____

MOST IMMEDIATE ACTION: _____

_____

_____

_____

_____

_____

LONG TERM GOAL: _____

_____

_____

_____

_____

_____

NOTES: _____

_____

_____

_____

▲

DATE: _____

PROBLEM: _____

_____

_____

QUESTION: _____

_____

_____

FIRST SELECTION: SOURCE _____

_____

_____

_____

_____

SECOND SELECTION: OBSTRUCTION _____

_____

_____

_____

_____

THIRD SELECTION: SOLUTION _____

_____

_____

_____

_____

M I N D   J O G G E R

MOST IMPORTANT DISCOVERY: _____

_____

_____

_____

_____

_____

MOST IMMEDIATE ACTION: _____

_____

_____

_____

_____

_____

LONG TERM GOAL: _____

_____

_____

_____

_____

_____

NOTES: _____

_____

_____

_____

▲

DATE: _____

PROBLEM: _____

_____

_____

QUESTION: _____

_____

_____

FIRST SELECTION: SOURCE _____

_____

_____

_____

_____

SECOND SELECTION: OBSTRUCTION _____

_____

_____

_____

_____

THIRD SELECTION: SOLUTION _____

_____

_____

_____

_____

M I N D J O G G E R

MOST IMPORTANT DISCOVERY: _____

_____

_____

_____

_____

_____

MOST IMMEDIATE ACTION: _____

_____

_____

_____

_____

_____

LONG TERM GOAL: _____

_____

_____

_____

_____

_____

NOTES: _____

_____

_____

_____

▲

DATE: _____

PROBLEM: _____

_____

_____

QUESTION: _____

_____

_____

FIRST SELECTION: SOURCE _____

_____

_____

_____

_____

SECOND SELECTION: OBSTRUCTION _____

_____

_____

_____

_____

THIRD SELECTION: SOLUTION _____

_____

_____

_____

_____

M I N D   J O G G E R

MOST IMPORTANT DISCOVERY: _____

_____

_____

_____

_____

_____

MOST IMMEDIATE ACTION: _____

_____

_____

_____

_____

_____

LONG TERM GOAL: _____

_____

_____

_____

_____

_____

NOTES: _____

_____

_____

_____

▲

DATE: _____

PROBLEM: _____

_____

_____

QUESTION: _____

_____

_____

FIRST SELECTION: SOURCE _____

_____

_____

_____

_____

SECOND SELECTION: OBSTRUCTION _____

_____

_____

_____

_____

THIRD SELECTION: SOLUTION _____

_____

_____

_____

_____

M I N D   J O G G E R

MOST IMPORTANT DISCOVERY: _____

_____

_____

_____

_____

_____

MOST IMMEDIATE ACTION: _____

_____

_____

_____

_____

_____

LONG TERM GOAL: _____

_____

_____

_____

_____

_____

NOTES: _____

_____

_____

_____

▲

DATE: _____

PROBLEM: _____

_____

_____

QUESTION: _____

_____

_____

FIRST SELECTION: SOURCE _____

_____

_____

_____

_____

SECOND SELECTION: OBSTRUCTION _____

_____

_____

_____

_____

THIRD SELECTION: SOLUTION _____

_____

_____

_____

_____

M I N D   J O G G E R

MOST IMPORTANT DISCOVERY: _____

_____

_____

_____

_____

_____

MOST IMMEDIATE ACTION: _____

_____

_____

_____

_____

_____

LONG TERM GOAL: _____

_____

_____

_____

_____

_____

NOTES: _____

_____

_____

_____

▲

DATE: _____

PROBLEM: _____

_____

_____

QUESTION: _____

_____

_____

FIRST SELECTION: SOURCE _____

_____

_____

_____

SECOND SELECTION: OBSTRUCTION _____

_____

_____

_____

THIRD SELECTION: SOLUTION _____

_____

_____

_____

_____

122

M I N D   J O G G E R

MOST IMPORTANT DISCOVERY: _____

_____

_____

_____

_____

_____

MOST IMMEDIATE ACTION: _____

_____

_____

_____

_____

_____

LONG TERM GOAL: _____

_____

_____

_____

_____

_____

NOTES: _____

_____

_____

_____

▲

DATE: _____

PROBLEM: _____

_____

_____

QUESTION: _____

_____

_____

FIRST SELECTION: SOURCE _____

_____

_____

_____

_____

SECOND SELECTION: OBSTRUCTION _____

_____

_____

_____

_____

THIRD SELECTION: SOLUTION _____

_____

_____

_____

_____

M I N D   J O G G E R

MOST IMPORTANT DISCOVERY: _____

_____

_____

_____

_____

_____

MOST IMMEDIATE ACTION: _____

_____

_____

_____

_____

_____

LONG TERM GOAL: _____

_____

_____

_____

_____

_____

NOTES: _____

_____

_____

_____

▲

DATE: _____

PROBLEM: _____

_____

_____

QUESTION: _____

_____

_____

FIRST SELECTION: SOURCE _____

_____

_____

_____

_____

SECOND SELECTION: OBSTRUCTION _____

_____

_____

_____

_____

THIRD SELECTION: SOLUTION _____

_____

_____

_____

_____

M I N D   J O G G E R

MOST IMPORTANT DISCOVERY: _____

_____

_____

_____

_____

_____

MOST IMMEDIATE ACTION: _____

_____

_____

_____

_____

_____

LONG TERM GOAL: _____

_____

_____

_____

_____

_____

NOTES: _____

_____

_____

_____

127

▲

DATE: _____

PROBLEM: _____

_____

_____

QUESTION: _____

_____

_____

FIRST SELECTION: SOURCE _____

_____

_____

_____

_____

SECOND SELECTION: OBSTRUCTION _____

_____

_____

_____

_____

THIRD SELECTION: SOLUTION _____

_____

_____

_____

_____

M I N D   J O G G E R

MOST IMPORTANT DISCOVERY: _____

_____

_____

_____

_____

_____

MOST IMMEDIATE ACTION: _____

_____

_____

_____

_____

_____

LONG TERM GOAL: _____

_____

_____

_____

_____

_____

NOTES: _____

_____

_____

_____

▲

DATE: _____

PROBLEM: _____

_____

_____

QUESTION: _____

_____

_____

FIRST SELECTION: SOURCE _____

_____

_____

_____

_____

SECOND SELECTION: OBSTRUCTION _____

_____

_____

_____

_____

THIRD SELECTION: SOLUTION _____

_____

_____

_____

_____

M I N D   J O G G E R

MOST IMPORTANT DISCOVERY: _____

_____

_____

_____

_____

MOST IMMEDIATE ACTION: _____

_____

_____

_____

_____

LONG TERM GOAL: _____

_____

_____

_____

_____

NOTES: _____

_____

_____

_____

▲

DATE: _____

PROBLEM: _____

_____

_____

QUESTION: _____

_____

_____

FIRST SELECTION: SOURCE _____

_____

_____

_____

_____

SECOND SELECTION: OBSTRUCTION _____

_____

_____

_____

_____

THIRD SELECTION: SOLUTION _____

_____

_____

_____

_____

M I N D   J O G G E R

MOST IMPORTANT DISCOVERY: _____

_____

_____

_____

_____

_____

MOST IMMEDIATE ACTION: _____

_____

_____

_____

_____

_____

LONG TERM GOAL: _____

_____

_____

_____

_____

_____

NOTES: _____

_____

_____

_____

▲

DATE: _____

PROBLEM: _____

_____

_____

QUESTION: _____

_____

_____

FIRST SELECTION: SOURCE _____

_____

_____

_____

_____

SECOND SELECTION: OBSTRUCTION _____

_____

_____

_____

_____

THIRD SELECTION: SOLUTION _____

_____

_____

_____

_____

M I N D　　J O G G E R

MOST IMPORTANT DISCOVERY: _____

_____

_____

_____

_____

_____

MOST IMMEDIATE ACTION: _____

_____

_____

_____

_____

_____

LONG TERM GOAL: _____

_____

_____

_____

_____

_____

NOTES: _____

_____

_____

_____

▲

DATE: _____

PROBLEM: _____

_____

_____

QUESTION: _____

_____

_____

FIRST SELECTION: SOURCE _____

_____

_____

_____

_____

SECOND SELECTION: OBSTRUCTION _____

_____

_____

_____

_____

THIRD SELECTION: SOLUTION _____

_____

_____

_____

_____

M I N D   J O G G E R

MOST IMPORTANT DISCOVERY: _____

_____

_____

_____

_____

_____

MOST IMMEDIATE ACTION: _____

_____

_____

_____

_____

_____

LONG TERM GOAL: _____

_____

_____

_____

_____

_____

NOTES: _____

_____

_____

_____

▲

DATE: _____

PROBLEM: _____

_____

_____

QUESTION: _____

_____

_____

FIRST SELECTION: SOURCE _____

_____

_____

_____

_____

SECOND SELECTION: OBSTRUCTION _____

_____

_____

_____

_____

THIRD SELECTION: SOLUTION _____

_____

_____

_____

_____

M I N D   J O G G E R

MOST IMPORTANT DISCOVERY: _____

_____

_____

_____

_____

_____

MOST IMMEDIATE ACTION: _____

_____

_____

_____

_____

_____

LONG TERM GOAL: _____

_____

_____

_____

_____

_____

NOTES: _____

_____

_____

_____

▲

DATE: _____

PROBLEM: _____

_____

_____

QUESTION: _____

_____

_____

FIRST SELECTION: SOURCE _____

_____

_____

_____

SECOND SELECTION: OBSTRUCTION _____

_____

_____

_____

THIRD SELECTION: SOLUTION _____

_____

_____

_____

_____

M I N D   J O G G E R

MOST IMPORTANT DISCOVERY: _____

_____

_____

_____

_____

_____

MOST IMMEDIATE ACTION: _____

_____

_____

_____

_____

_____

LONG TERM GOAL: _____

_____

_____

_____

_____

_____

NOTES: _____

_____

_____

_____

▲

AN
ANNOTATED
BIBLIOGRAPHY

The following books have influenced my writing of Mind Jogger.
I have made brief comments after each book title, telling
why each book was important to me, realizing that
readers may wish to fill in some of the gaps I might have
left in Mind Jogger in the interest of economy.

The Aquarian Conspiracy, by Marilyn Ferguson, published by
J.P. Tarcher/Houghton Mifflin Co., 1980. This book has
probably done more than any other single book of our
time to support those of us, in every walk of life, who
look upon our work in life as a personal adventure and
who believe that our individual progress in this adventure
matters.

The Basic Writings of C.G. Jung, edited by V.S. de Laszlo,
published by The Modern Library, 1959. This little collection of Jung's writings has traveled with me for nearly 25
years. It is always interesting for me to pick up this book
and again read an essay that seemed so abstruse to me
a decade or two ago but which seems like "common
knowledge" to me today. I am especially grateful to Jung
for introducing concepts such as the collective unconscious
and synchronicity which allowed me to see that we are
all connected with the past and the future by universal
threads that give us greater strength and greater responsibilities than most of us can quite accept or imagine.

The Farther Reaches of Human Nature, by Abraham Maslow,
published by The Viking Press, 1979. Maslow's work on
the peak experience and the nature of creativity made me
realize, for the first time, that our greatest efforts should be
directed not at "correcting" what we perceived as our
personal shortcomings but at creating tools to move forward, exploring our individual uniqueness and what it
has to offer. It was through Maslow's work that I first
came to see that there was a difference between correcting disease and creating health, which has been the central theme of my work with Mike Samuels, my co-author
on several health books over the years. In writing Mind
Jogger I again owe a debt to Maslow in providing the
philosophical "template" for keeping the readings regen-
erative rather than corrective.

▲

The I CHING. This ancient classic, literally translated as "The Book of Changes," has assisted millions and millions of people, in both Eastern and Western cultures, through difficult decisions and changes. Attributed to Fu Hsi, the legendary ruler of China somewhere around the third millennium B.C., it was first most widely used as a farming, fishing, and hunting almanac. Since then it has been edited, rewritten, and revised thousands of times over the millennia, now reflecting the human wisdom that includes a greater span in time than the Bible, incorporating the thoughts of great political, religious, and philosophical leaders of the Asian culture, providing guidance that can be useful to any person in any society or vocation.

MAKING SELECTIONS WITH CARDS

You may prefer to use cards rather than the 20-sided die to select Mind Jogger readings. You can use ordinary playing cards or a Tarot deck.

To make selections with an ordinary deck of playing cards, use only the Ace, Deuce, Jack, Queen, and King from the four suits.

To make selections with the Rider Waite Tarot deck, use only the Ace, Deuce, Page, Queen, and King of Swords, Cups, Pentacles, and Wands.

Shuffle this short deck and select three cards, just as you would cast the die three times to make your reading selections. Other than changing the method of selecting the readings, all other instructions, as described on pages 24 to 33 are the same.

The charts here cross-reference the cards and their suits with the numbered readings.

ORDINARY DECK

	♠	♥	♦	♣
ACE	1	6	11	16
DEUCE	2	7	12	17
JACK	3	8	13	18
QUEEN	4	9	14	19
KING	5	10	15	20
		Reading Selections		

TAROT DECK

	🗡	🏆	⬟	🪄
ACE	1	6	11	16
DEUCE	2	7	12	17
PAGE	3	8	13	18
QUEEN	4	9	14	19
KING	5	10	15	20
		Reading Selections		

ABOUT THE AUTHOR

Hal Zina Bennett is the co-author, with Mike Samuels, M.D., of **Spirit Guides: Access to Inner Worlds,** and the pioneering holistic health manual, **The Well Body Book.** He also co-authored **Peak Performance: Mental Training Techniques of the World's Greatest Athletes,** with Charles Garfield.

Hal Bennett is the creator of PATH: Inner Resources, a system of tools for teaching people how to identify and apply their own inner resources (intuition, creativity, the "screen of consciousness," and psychic capabilities). He is an inner resource instructor, offering short- and long-term individual consultations and group seminars. Write the author for more information about PATH: Inner Resources.

NOTE: Mind Jogger is also available as a software program for most popular home computer systems. Write the author for more information:

Hal Zina Bennett
P.O. Box 60655
Palo Alto, CA 94306

A WORD FROM THE PUBLISHER

Celestial Arts publishes books in the areas of self-help, spirituality, awareness and consciousness, New Age, cookery, California Cuisine, health, and fitness. For a complete list of our publications please write for our free catalog or call (415) 524-1801. Our address is P.O. Box 7327, Berkeley, CA 94707.

Celestial Arts is a part of the total publishing program of Ten Speed Press, publishers of career and life guidance books such as **What Color Is Your Parachute?** Ten Speed Press also publishes a distinguished line of cookbooks and books in the areas of business, reference, outdoors, housecrafts, lifestyle, and mischief. For Ten Speed's free catalog, please write or phone (415) 845-8414. Ten Speed Press, P.O. Box 7123, Berkeley, CA 94707.